MW00577354

ACLS History E-Book Project
Reprint Series

The ACLS History E-Book Project (www.historyebook.org) collaborates with constituent societies of the American Council of Learned Societies, publishers, librarians and historians to create an electronic collection of works of high quality in the field of history. This volume is produced from digital images created for the Project by the Scholarly Publishing Office and the Digital Library Production Service at the University of Michigan, Ann Arbor. The digital reformatting process results in an electronic version of the text that can be both accessed online and used to create new print copies. This book and hundreds of others are available online in the History E-Book Project through subscription.

Many of the works in the History E-Book Project are available in print and can be ordered either directly from their publishers or as part of this series. For information refer to the online Title Record page for each book. Inquiries regarding this series can be directed to info@hebook.org.

ACLS
HISTORY E-BOOK

http://www.historyebook.org

JAVA IN THE 14TH CENTURY

NĀGARA-KĚRTĀGAMA

VOLUME I

A POET, V. PAGE V.

KONINKLIJK INSTITUUT
VOOR TAAL-, LAND- EN VOLKENKUNDE
TRANSLATION SERIES 4, 1

&

JAVA IN THE 14TH CENTURY

A STUDY IN CULTURAL HISTORY

THE NĀGARA-KĔRTĀGAMA BY *RAKAWI*

PRAPAÑCA OF MAJAPAHIT, 1365 A.D.

Third edition, revised and enlarged by some contemporaneous texts,
with notes, translations, commentaries and a glossary

by

THEODORE G. Tн. PIGEAUD, Pн. D. Leyden

Illustrated with drawings by Professor Tн. P. GALESTIN

PUBLICATION COMMISSIONED AND FINANCED BY
THE NETHERLANDS INSTITUTE FOR INTERNATIONAL CULTURAL RELATIONS

I

JAVANESE TEXTS IN TRANSCRIPTION

THE HAGUE - MARTINUS NIJHOFF - 1960

The complete work is in five volumes:

VOLUME I

TABLE OF CONTENTS

PREFACE

The panegyrical poem called Nāgara-Kĕrtāgama, written in honour of King Hayam Wuruk of the Eastern Javanese kingdom of Majapahit, is hereby for the first time published with an English translation. As it is a most important source of information on 14th century Javanese civilization the Directors of the *Koninklijk Instituut voor Taal-, Land- en Volkenkunde* (Royal Institute of Ethnology) of The Hague have deserved well of scholars not conversant with the Dutch language by making this edition available. By providing funds for the publication the Netherlands Institute for International Cultural Relations has placed all students of things Javanese under an obligation. The present author is indebted to Professor de Josselin de Jong jr of Leyden for advice on the English idiom, and to Professor Galestin, also of Leyden, for providing drawings made after 14th century Javanese reliefs to serve as illustrations.

Leyden, 1960.

INTRODUCTION

I. *The Text of the Nāgara-Kĕrtāgama.*

The old-Javanese manuscript written on palm-leaves, now known as Codex Orientalis 5023 of the Legatum Warnerianum, Leyden University Library, was discovered on the 18th of November 1894 by Dr J. Brandes in the palace-compound of the Balinese King of Cakra Nĕgara, on the island of Lombok, one of the Lesser Sunda Islands to the east of Bali. By order of the Governor-General of the Netherlands East Indies, Dr Brandes, then Government linguist, was attached to the staff of the military forces engaged in the Lombok war, with a view to preserve from destruction all objects of cultural interest to be found, especially manuscripts. At that time it was already a well-known fact that the best manuscripts of Old Javanese, i.e. pre-Muslim, literature are to be found in the libraries of the Balinese Kings, nobles and priests who adhere to their peculiar form of Javanistic Hinduism, whereas the majority of the Javanese turned Muslim in the 15th and 16th centuries and subsequently forgot most of their ancient arts and letters. The discovery of the Nāgara-Kĕrtāgama manuscript was a fair reward of Dr Brandes' efforts.

Codex 5023 includes yet some more Old Javanese texts as well. The Lubdhaka kakawin and the Kuñjarakarṇa kakawin are of considerable interest.

In 1902 Dr Brandes published the Nāgara-Kĕrtāgama text in the *Verhandelingen van het Bataviaasch Genootschap van Kunsten en Wetenschappen,* vol. 54. Perhaps the delay in publishing so valuable a text was partly caused by the expected discovery of yet another manuscript of the Nāgara-Kĕrtāgama in the collections at Batavia (Djakarta) and at Leyden, which were enriched at that time by many new acquisitions. But neither then nor at any later period has another manuscript of the Nāgara-Kĕrtāgama been discovered. Codex 5023 is unique.

It is worth mentioning that the Nāgara-Kĕrtāgama text of codex 5023 has drawn the attention of a Balinese reader. He was especially interested in those passages where the island of Bali is mentioned and in the description of a Court festival in Majapahit. He added short notes in the margins of the leaves that contain those passages, apparently in order to enable him to find them again. Probably the preservation of the 14th century Nāgara-Kĕrtāgama text in the 18th century Cakra Nĕgara palace library was due to the Balinese nobility's interest in texts referring to the age-old connection between the Majapahit and the Bali Royal Courts.

Dr Brandes caused the Nāgara-Kĕrtāgama text to be printed in Balinese characters as nearly as possible in conformity to the original manuscript. He did not supply a translation or a commentary. Dr Brandes found the name Nāgara-Kĕrtāgama in Cod. Or. 5023 in a Balinese scribe's colophon appended to the text. He took it for the true name of the poem, and so it has been called by scholars ever since. However, the Javanese author who lived in the 14th century at the Majapahit Court probably called his poem *Deça-Warṇana* (Desha-Warṇana), Description of the Country.

Professor Kern, of Leyden, then, in his old age, shouldered the heavy task of studying the Nāgara-Kĕrtāgama text in order to provide a translation and a commentary. As his work advanced he published, from 1903 to 1914, canto after canto in romanized transcription, with a translation and a commentary in Dutch. The first cantos appeared in *De Indische Gids,* the following in the *Bijdragen tot de Taal-, Land- en Volkenkunde van Nederlandsch-Indië,* both at The Hague. In 1917/'18 these translations were combined to produce the first complete edition of the text, published in the *Verspreide Geschriften* (Collected Works) of Professor Kern, vol. VII and VIII, under the title: *Het Oud-Javaansche Lofdicht Nāgarakṛtāgama van Prapañca, 1365 A.D.*

Unlike Dr Brandes' edition, in Professor Kern's book the transcribed text has been subjected to editing. Professor Kern made many emendations in order to re-establish the original text as written by the author. These emendations are not always clearly indicated in notes. Thus the transcribed text does not faithfully reproduce the text of codex 5023.

After publishing Professor Kern's Collected Works, the Directors of the Royal Institute thought fit to offer a separate edition of the Nāgara-Kĕrtāgama to the public. In 1919 Professor Krom, of Leyden, was found willing to take care of this edition. With the whole-hearted approval of the Directors he availed himself of the opportunity to append in the form of notes everything he thought of use for the better understanding of the text. These appendices, divided into (*a*) notes on the text and (*b*) explanatory notes, considerably enhanced the value of the reprint of Professor Kern's translation. Professor Krom's work may justly be considered as a second, revised and enlarged edition.

In the notes on the text, Krom, continuing the work of Kern, indicated with the utmost accuracy wherever he found the text of codex 5023 needed emendation, especially in connexion with the metre. In the explanatory notes he inserted many emendations proposed by himself and other scholars.

Professor Krom's edition, with its appendices, was not an easy book to handle. Nevertheless it has been in use since 1919. In the course of time several scholars proposed emendations and new translations. The Notes (*Aanteekeningen op de Nāgarakṛtāgama, Bijdragen K. Instituut, 80, 1924*) of the Javanese scholar Professor *Raden Mas Ngabehi* Dr Poerbatjaraka are most valuable in this respect. It gave a great deal of trouble and it took much time, though, to consult them continually when studying the text.

In 1948 the Directors of the Royal Institute entrusted the present author with the preparation of a completely new edition of the Nāgara-Kĕrtāgama, Professor Krom's book being out of print. He has found it the best plan to reproduce the text of codex 5023, till now the only available text, in a faithful transcription. The emendations, proposed by his predecessors and by himself, are relegated to the *Notes on the Text and the Translations* in Vol. II. In this way it will be easier than before to form a correct idea of the quality of the text and to compare the proposed emendations and translations as to their respective merits.

II. *The Minor Writings and the Charters.*

The present edition contains some smaller Javanese texts and several charters contemporaneous with the Nāgara-Kĕrtāgama, most of them now for the first time translated and annotated. They have been chosen for their usefulness in providing explanations of technical terms of law and religion found in the major poem. The present author regrets that limitations of space did not allow him to increase the number of these smaller writing and charters. The codices of the Leyden University Library, and the books by other authors which contain these texts are indicated in the *Notes on the Texts and the Translations* in the second volume of the present edition.

Moreover, in the fourth volume, following the commentaries on the Nāgara-Kĕrtāgama, the minor writings and the charters, several chapters containing general discussions of subjects of cultural interest of the Majapahit period, mainly sociological, have been added as a recapitulation of results. History and archeology have profited already by the thorough discussions by Kern, Krom and others of the Nāgara-Kĕrtāgama passages that are of importance in these respects. The results of those discussions are common property of historians and archeologists. It is hoped that the present Nāgara-Kĕrtāgama edition with its appendices may be found to contain some new facts that should be of special interest to students of sociology and cultural anthropology.

III. The Transcription.

The system used for transcribing the Balinese characters of the Nāgara-Kĕrtāgama manuscript is the usual one, introduced by Professor Kern. Keeping as close as possible to the orthography of codex 5023, the present author has *not* followed Kern's example in intercalating an ĕ in all those cases where the metre seemed to require it, between consonants that are written as ligatures in the original, nor in substituting *dh* for *ḍ* to be in accordance with Sanskrit orthography. On the other hand the *kh* is transcribed faithfully every time it is used in the manuscript. Both Brandes and Kern have neglected the *kh*.

The Javanese *wigñan*, the Balinese *bisah* at the end of a syllable is transcribed as *ḥ*. The vocalic *ḷ* and *ṛ* always are transcribed as *ḷ* and *ṛ*. (Kern substitutes sometimes *lĕ* and *rĕ*, in other places *ĕl* and *ĕr*, according to the exigencies of the metre). The Javanese and Balinese *cĕcak* at the end of a syllable is transcribed as *ŋ*, the guttural nasal written as *akṣara* as *ṅ*, in accordance with the system of Dr de Casparis in his publications on Old Javanese charters (*Prasasti Indonesia*, Bandung 1950). In the *Translation* and the *Commentaries*, however, common *ng* is used. In the *Glossary* (vol. V) the standard transcription is *ŋ*.

The Javanese and Balinese *paten*, separating two *akṣaras*, is transcribed as /. Two consonants not separated by / in the transcription must be considered as forming a ligature in the manuscript. The end of a verse, in the manuscript indicated by a small sloping line and a *paten*, if necessary, is only marked by a comma in the transcription. The *pada*, marking the end of a stanza, is transcribed as a full stop. The place of the double *pada*, marking the end of a canto and the beginning of a new one, with another metre, is indicated in the transcription by a final dash.

Neither capitals nor punctuation have been used in the transcription, both being non-existant in the manuscript. The words are separated by space in the usual manner, though. Without this separation of words the transcription would have offered too singular an aspect. The cantos have been numbered and the name and scheme of the metre have been prefixed te each, according to the list in Professor Krom's edition.

The handwriting of the Nāgara-Kĕrtāgama copy in codex 5023 in the well-known Balinese Old Javanese script is sufficiently clear, but not handsome. Without any doubt the copy contains many mistakes, in the first place offences against the Indian metrics. The number of mistakes of this kind indicated by Kern and Krom is considerable. One is led to suppose that the scribe (or his predecessors) had no clear apprehension of the difference between short and long syllables in Indian prosody. Long vowels are frequently written in the following cases: at the end of a verse, if it is open, and in titles and names of persons of high rank, to show respect, and sometimes in syllables that are long by position. Just like the Javanese scribes of the 17th century, the Balinese mainly distinguished the Indian metres by counting the syllables in one verse, irrespective of their quantity. This is apparent, moreover, from the fact that the scribe (or one of his predecessors) in some cases failed to insert a double *pada,* indicating a change of the metre. This occurs where the verses of two consecutive cantos have (approximately) the same number of syllables. The difference of the metres apparently escaped the scribe's observation.

The scribe of codex 5023 (or one of his predecessors) uses aspirates (especially *jh* in *Majhapahit,* sometimes *kh*) and *ṇ* instead of *n* in titles and names, to show respect. The authentic value of the *akṣaras* was forgotten. The Javanese scribes from the 18th century onward have made a rule of it to use aspirates in this fashion. They take the place of capitals to indicate names.

In addition to offences against Indian metrics and Sanskrit ortho-graphy, the scribe of codex 5023 made many more mistakes (or he transmitted mistakes made by his predecessors). The text shows many verses containing too few or too many syllables. In one instance a whole verse is missing. Several passages are incomprehensible, they must be corrupt. One is led to suppose that the scribe had a rather small understanding of the meaning of some parts of the text. This is apparent, moreover, from some cases of queer spelling and most unusual linking of words.

The scribe was not unaware of the deficiences of his work. In some cases he left some space open for an *akṣara* in the text of his predecessor he could not read. In several instances he eliminated *akṣaras* he thought amiss by putting dots above and below them. The text shows some later interpolations of *akṣaras* that were inadvertently omitted in the first writing. The interpolated *akṣaras* are written under the line, accompanied by a reference-mark between the *akṣaras* concerned in the emendation.

All the scribe's interpolations and emendations are to be found in the transcription and the notes of the present edition.

As has been mentioned above, Kern and Krom have tried to reconstruct the original text of the Nāgara-Kĕrtāgama, as written by the author. Without any doubt the original text must have been more pure, both in respect of metrics and of orthography, than the text of codex 5023. It is debatable, however, whether it was without flaws. One may surmise that in the 14th century the Javanese literati's knowledge of Sanskrit grammar was not so thorough that they never erred. For that reason reconstructing the original text is to be considered a precarious enterprise. The present author has preferred, therefore, to transcribe faithfully the only text of the Nāgara-Kĕrtāgama that has been handed down to us, such as it is. He has thought it superfluous to take into account the edition of the text published by Brandes. That edition shows mistakes by which Kern occasionally was led astray.

The texts of the minor writings Nawanatya and Rājapatiguṇḍala that are appended to the present Nāgara-Kĕrtāgama edition have been transcribed from manuscripts of the Leyden University Library mentioned in the *Notes on the Texts and the Translation*. In the transcription the same rules as in the case of the major poem have been observed. On the other hand the texts of the other minor writings and the charters have been copied from former editions, also mentioned in the *Notes*. As a rule in their case the usual romanized orthography for Javanese texts has been retained.

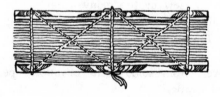

A JAVANESE BOOK, V. PAGE V.

NĀGARA-KĚRTĀGAMA

TEXT

CHAPTER 1 - THE ROYAL FAMILY.

Canto 1.

Metre: - - - ◡ ◡ - ◡ - ◡ ◡ ◡ - ◡ ◡ ◡ ◡ ◡ - - ◡ - ◡ e
23 feet, jagaddhita.

(92a) awighnam āstu.

1. oṃ nāthāya namostu te stutiniṅ atpada ri pada bhaṭāra nityaça,
saṅ sūkṣmeṅ tlĕṅ iṅ samādi çiwa budda *(92b)* sira sakala niṣkalātmakā,
saṅ çrī parwwatanātha nāthaniṅ anātha sira ta patiniṅ jagatpati,
saṅ hyaṅ niṅ hyaṅ iniṣṭy acintyaniṅ acintya hanā waya tmahnireṅ
[jagat.
2. byāpi byāpaka sarwwatatwagata niguṇa sira riṅ apakṣa weṣṇawa,
riṅ yogīçwara poruṣeṅ kapila jambhala sakala sirān/ hyaṅ iṅ dana,
çrī wāgindra sirān hyaṅ iṅ sakalaçāstra manasija sireṅ smarāgama,
riṅ wighnotsarana prayoga yamarāja sira makapalaṅ jagaddita.

3. nāhan don iṅ umastutī padanirāhyun umikĕta kate nareçwara,
saṅ çrī nātha ri wilwatikta haji rājasanagara wiçeṣa bhūpāti,
sākṣat/ janma bhaṭāra nātha siran aṅhilaṅakĕn i kalaṅkaniṅ prajā,
hĕntyaṅ bhūmi jawātibhakti manukūla tumuluy i tkeṅ digantara.

4. riṅ çāka rttu çarena rakwa ri wijil/ nṛpati tlas inastwakĕn/ prabhū,
an/ garbbheçwara nātha riṅ kawuripan/ wihaganiran amānuṣādbhūta,
linduṅ bhūmi ktug hudan hawu gĕṛh kilat awiltan iṅ nabhastala,
guntur ttaṅ himawān/ ri kāmpud ananaṅ kujana kuhaka māti
[tanpagap.
5. nāhan/ hiṅanirān bhaṭāra girinātha sakala matmah prabhūttama,
na lwir sādĕgirekanaṅ sayawabhūmi cawa tluk umungku *(93a)* l ādara,
wipra kṣatriya waiçya çūdra catur açrama sama nipuṇeṅ samāhitā,
hĕntyaṅ dūrjjana maryyābuddi kala kewala matakut i wiryya saṅ
[prabhū.

Canto 2.

Metre: - - - - ◡ - - - ◡ ◡ ◡ ◡ ◡ - - - ◡ - - - ◡ ๏
21 feet, sragdharā.

1. ndan/ saŋ çrī rājapatni prakaçita sira mātāmahā çri narendra,
saŋ lwir pāwak/ bhaṭāri paramabhagawati catraniñ rāt/ wiçeṣa,
utsāheŋ yoga buddasmaraṇa ginĕñirān/ cīwari wṛddamuṇḍi,
riŋ çāka dṛṣṭi sāptāruṇa kalahanirān/ mokta muŋsir kkabuddan.

2. ryyantuk/ çrī rājapatnī jinapada kawkas/ duḥkitañ rāt byamoha,
ryyādĕg/ çrī nātha muṅgwiŋ majhapahit umuluy/ tuṣṭa maṅgöŋ
[kabhaktin,
reṇa çrī nātha saŋ çrī tribhūwana jīwayottuṅgal dewi gumanti,
muṅgwiŋ rājyerikaŋ jīwanapura sira tāmwaŋmwañ i çrī narendra.

———

Canto 3.

Metre: - - - ◡ ◡ - ◡ - ◡ ◡ ◡ - - - ◡ - - ◡ ๏
19 feet, çārdūlawikrīḍita.

1. tĕkwan bhakti sirān makebu ri sira çrī rājapatniçwari,
satyānūt/ brata pakṣa sogata masaŋskāre dagan saŋ pjaḥ,
tan saḥ çrī kṛtawarddaneçwara pitā de çrī narendrādipa,
sedampatyapagĕḥ sireŋ sugatamārggañde sukhaniŋ jagat.

2. ndan/ çrī bhūpati saŋ pitā nṛpati muṅgwiŋ siṅhasāryy apagĕḥ,
sākṣāt/ hyaŋ wawa ratnasambhawa sirān māṅgĕḥ parārttaŋ ja
[(93b)gat,
ḍirotsāha sire kadṛḍḍyanikanaŋ rāt/ satya bhaktye haji,
lagyāṅgĕgwani karyya sahana kāḍyakṣātidakṣeŋ naya.

———

Canto 4.

Metre: ◡ ◡ ◡ ◡ ◡ ◡ - ◡ - - ◡ - - ◡ - - ◡ ๏
18 feet, mahāmālikā.

1. muwah ibu haji saŋ narendrānujā de hajīŋ jiwana,
prakaçita haji rājadewī mahārājasānindita,
sira ta siniwi riŋ dāha nopameŋ pariŋ sadguṇa,
samasa kalawan hajiŋ jiwana lwir sudewyāpaliḥ.

2. priya haji saṅ umuṅgwiŋ weṅkĕr baṅun hyaṅ upendrānurun,
   nṛpati wijaya rājasānopameŋ paramajñottama,
   samasama kalawan/ nṛpati siṅhasāryyakapakṣāpa . . .
   sira wihikan iŋ thāni yāwat/ sabhūmī jawa.

Canto 5.

Metre: – – – ᴗ ᴗ ᴗ ᴗ – – – ᴗ – ◦
13 feet, praharṣinī.

1. wwantĕn tāri haji ri wilwatikta rājñi,
   saŋ muṅgwiŋ lasĕm anuraga riŋ kahaywan,
   putrī çrī narapati riŋ dahā prakāça,
   saŋ çrī rājasa duhitendu dewyanindya.

2. ndan çrī warddana duhiteçwari pamuṅsu,
   rājñī muṅgwiŋ pajaṅ anopameŋ raras rūm,
   putrī çrī nṛpati ri jīwana prakāça,
   an/ sākṣāt anuja tkapniraŋ narendrā.

Canto 6.

Metre: – – – ᴗ ᴗ – ᴗ – ᴗ ᴗ ᴗ – – – ᴗ – – ᴗ ◦
19 feet, çārdūlawikrīḍita.

1. penan/ çrī naranātha kapwa ta huwus/ labḍa bhiṣeka prabhū,
   saŋ nātheŋ matahun/ priya nṛpati saŋ rājyeŋ lasĕm/ suçrama
   saŋ çrī rājasa warddana prakaçiteŋ rūpā (94a) ḍi wijñeŋ naya,
   tan pendaḥ smarapiṅgalā patĕmu saŋ nāthenalm niŋ jagat.

2. saŋ nātheŋ paguhan/ priya nṛpati saŋ rājī pratiṣṭe pajaŋ,
   kyātī çrī nṛpa siṅhawarddana surūpānwam/ suçilāpagĕḥ,
   açry āwarṇna sanatkumāra saha dewiḍā papaṅgihnira,
   bhaktī jöŋ haji māsih awwaṅ anak aṅde tuṣṭani nāgara.

3. těkwan/ wṛddyawke narendrā saŋ umuṅgwiŋ wirabhūmy aṇḍiri,
    saŋ çrī nāgarawarddani pratīta rājñī kānyakānopama,
    ndan/ rantěn/ haji rāja ratwiŋ mataram/ lwir hyaŋ kumārānurun,
    saŋ çrī wikramawarddaneçwara paniṅkah çrī narendrāḍipa.

4. wuṅsu çrī nṛpati pajaŋ siniwi muŋgwi pawwanawwan/ purī,
    rājñī çrī surawarddanī nwamira wāla lwir hajěŋ niŋ tulis,
    sakweh çrī yaja ¹ rāja sapaḍa madudwan nagarātuṅgalan,
    ekhasthāna ri wilwatikta maṅisapwī saŋ narendrāḍipa.

———

Canto 7.

Metre: - - - ‿ ‿ - ‿ - ‿ ‿ ‿ - ‿ ‿ ‿ ‿ ‿ ‿ - ‿ - ‿ ●
23 feet, jagaddhita.

1. warṇnan/ çrī naranātha kastawaniran dinakharasama digjaya
                                        [prabhū,
    bhraṣṭaŋ çatru baṅun tamiçra sahane bhūwana rinawasan nareçwara,
    tuṣṭā sajjana paṅajamam ikanaṅ kujana kumuda satya satwikā,
    sthityaŋ ghrāma sabhūmy aweh ḍana baṅun/ jala hinaturakěn/ ya
                                        [sakrama.
2. lwir saŋ hyaŋ ça- *(94b)* tamanyu maṅhudani rāt/ haji tumulak i
                                        [dūhkhaniŋ prajā,
    lwir hyaŋ pitṛpati kaḍaṇḍaniṅ anāryya baruṇa ri katmwaniŋ ḍana,
    lwir hyaŋ bāyu sirān tameŋ sakalaloka makaçaraṇa dūta nityaça,
    lwir pṛthwi ri karakṣaniŋ pura katonanira kadi bhaṭāra candramā.

3. riŋ warṇnakṛti kāmadewa sakalānurun umulat i rāmyaniŋ purī,
    sakweh saŋ para putrikādika waḍū haji kadi pawibhajyaniŋ ratih,
    ndan saŋ çrī parameçwari swaduhitā nṛpati wijayarājasottama,
    mukyāwarṇna susumnadewy anūpameŋ hayu tuhu sawawe
                                        [nareçwara.
4. těkwan/ wṛddi sirān/ pakānak i siraŋ nṛpati kusumawarddanīçwarī,
    rājī rājakumāryy anindya siniwi pura ri kabalan utameŋ raras,
    saŋ çrī wikramawarddanendra saniruktyanira paṅucapiŋ sanāgara,
    sākṣāt/ dewata dewati sirān atmwa hlam anukani twasiŋ jagat.

———

¹ corrected by the scribe: *wa.*

CHAPTER 2 - THE CAPITAL.

Canto 8.

Metre: - - - ᵛ ᵛ - ᵛ - ᵛ ᵛ ᵛ - ᵛ ᵛ ᵛ ᵛ ᵛ ᵛ - - - ᵛ ᵛ ᵛ ᵛ ᵛ
25 feet, a kind of atikṛti.

1. wārṇnan tiṅkah ikaŋ purādbhuta kuthanya bata baṅ umidĕr
    [mmakandĕl aruhur,
    kulwan/ ḍi dwura waktra maṅharpakan ḷbuh agĕṅ i tṅah way
    [edran adaḷm,
    brāhmāsthāna matuṅgalan pathani buḍḍi jajar inapi kapwa sök
    [caracara,
    ṅkā (95a) toṅgwan para taṇḍa tan pgat aganti kumĕmit i
    [karakṣaniŋ purasabhā.

2. lor ttaŋ gopura çobhitābhinawa kontĕn ika wsi rinūpakāparimitā,
    wetan/ saṇḍiṅ ikārjja paṅguṅ aruhur/ patigan ika binajralepa
    [maputiḥ,
    kānnaḥ lor kkidul i pkĕn/ rakĕt ikaŋ yaça wkasiṅ apañjaṅ
    [adbhuta dahāt,
    aṅkĕn/ caitra pahömaniŋ bala samūha kidūl ika catuspathāhyaṅ
    [ahaḷp.

3. alwāgimbar ikaŋ waṅuntur an haturddiçi wataṅan ikāwitāna ri tṅah,
    lor ttaŋ weçma panaṅkilan/ para bhūjaṅga khimuta para mantry
    [aliṅgih apupul,
    wetan/ ṅgwan para çewa boḍḍa mawiwāda mucap aji sahopakāra
    [wki sök,
    prāyaççitta ri kālaniṅ grahaṇa phalguṇa makaphala haywaniŋ
    [sabhūwana.

4. kānnaḥ wetan ikaŋ pahoman ajajar ttiga tiga ri tṅah kaçaiwan
    [aruhur,
    ṅgwan saŋ wipra kidul paḍottama susun/ barat i natar ikābatur
    [patawuran,
    ṅgwan saŋ sogata lor susun tiga tikaŋ waṅunan i pucak ārjja
    [mokirukiran,
    kapwāṅjraḥ racananya puspa pinaran/ nṛpati satata yan hanoma
    [mapupul.

5. ṅkāneṋ jro kiduliṋ wañuntur ahḷt/ palawañan ika (95b) na
   [paçewan atathā,
   weçmārjjājajar aṅhapit hawan añulwan i tñah ika tañjuṅ aṋjrah
   [askar,
   ndaḥ kulwan/ mahḷt mūwaḥ kidul i paṅguṅ ika balay aneka
   [medran i tpi,
   arḍḍālwā ri tñaḥ natar nikana maṇḍapa pasatan açaṅkya lot
   [mawurahan.

6. rī jronyeki muwaḥ paçewan akidul/ dudug añusi wijil kapiṋrwa
   [ri daḷm,
   tiṅkaḥnyeki tinumpatumpa mahḷt/ palawañan ikanaṋ sapaṇta
   [tiniṅkaḥ,
   kapwa wweçma subadḍa watwan ika len/ saka balabag usuknya
   [tanpacacadan,
   sök deniṋ bala hajy anaṅkil agilir/ makmit an umapekṣa wāra
   [matutur.

Canto 9.

Metre: – – – – ᴗ – – ᴗ ᴗ ᴗ ᴗ ᴗ – – – ᴗ – – – ᴗ – ᴗ
21 feet, sragdharā.

1. nāhan lwirnyaṋ manaṅkil pañalasan iñaran/ kweḥnya tanpa pramāṇa,
   tanpalwir nyū gaḍiṋ jaṅgala kaḍiri sḍaḥ pañlaraṅ rājadewī,
   waiçaṅkā wwaṋ panewwan/ kṛtapura sinlir mwaṋ jayeṋ praṋ
   [jayāgöṋ,
   aṅreyok kaywapu wwaṋ jalaḍi pasuruhan/ sāmajāḍi prakirṇna.

2. nāhan tāḍinya muṅgwiṋ watañan alunalun tan/ pgat lot maganti,
   taṇḍa mwaṋ gusti wadwā haji muwah ikaṅ amwaṋ tuhan/ riṋ
   [yawābāp,
   mukyaṋ muṅgwiṋ wijil/ pi kalih aḍika bhayaṅkāryyapintāpu-
   (96a) pul/ sök,
   lor niṋ dwāre daḷm/ ṅgwanya kidul ika para kṣatriya mwaṋ
   [bhūjaṅgā.

3. ṅkāneṋ bāyabya ri paççima miděr umāreṋ mṛtyūdeça yaçākweḥ,
   sar sök de saṋ sumantryāmawa pinituha riṋ wirabhṛtyān panaṅkil,
   anyat kannaḥ kidul/ pāntaran ika lawañan/ maṇḍapa mwaṋ
   [gṛhākweḥ,
   sar sök de bhṛtya sa çrī nṛpati ri paguhan nītyakālan paçewa.

4. ṅkāne jroniŋ wijil piŋ kalih arja natarnyāratālwātiçobha,
   sök/ weçma mwaŋ witanābhinawa papupulan/ saŋ manaṅkil
   [mareŋ jro,
   wetan tekaŋ grhānopama waṅunan ikāçry aruhur sopacara,
   ṅgwan/ çrī nāthan paweh çewa riṅ umarĕk umuṅgwiŋ
   [witanāprameya.

Canto 10.

Metre: – – – ᴗ ᴗ – ᴗ – ᴗ ᴗ ᴗ – ᴗ – ᴗ ᴗ ᴗ ᴗ ᴖ
18 feet, a kind of dhṛti.

1. warṇnan/ warṇna ni saŋ manaṅkil irikaŋ witānā satatā,
   mantrī wṛdḍa parāryya len para pasaṅguhan/ sakapark,
   mwaŋ saŋ pañca ri wilwatikta mapagĕḥ dmuŋ kanuruhān,
   tansaḥ raṅga tumĕṅguṅ uttama ni saŋ mark/ wki pnuḥ.

2. kweh niŋ weçapurī kamantryan iṅ amātya riŋ sanāgara,
   doniŋ bhāṣa parāpatiḥ pāra dmuŋ sakalan apupul,
   aṅhiŋ saŋ juruniŋ watĕk/ paṅalasan/ mahīṅan apagöḥ,
   pañcākwehnira mantry anindi- (96b) ta rumakṣa kāryya ri daḷm.

3. ndan/ saŋ kṣatriya len/ bhujaṅga rṣi wipra yapwan umark,
   ṅkāne höbniṅ açokha muṅgwi hiriṅiŋ witānā maṅadĕg,
   ḍarmmādyakṣa kalih lawan/ saṅ upapatti sapta dulur,
   saŋ tuhw āryya lkasnirān/ paṅaran āryya yukti satirun.

Canto 11.

Metre: – – – ᴗ ᴗ – ᴗ – ᴗ ᴗ ᴗ – ᴗ ᴗ ᴗ ᴗ ᴗ – ᴗ – ᴗ ᴖ
23 feet, jagaddhita.

1. nā lwir saŋ mark iŋ witāna pinake daḷm inapi rinaṅga çobhitā,
   riŋ jro pūrwwa sake wijil/ pisan adoḥ pininit ikaṅ umañjiṅe daḷm,
   ndan saŋ çrī nrpati siṅhawardḍana kidul/ saha yugāla saputraputrīkā,
   lor saŋ çrī krtawardḍaneçwara baṅun/ surapada tiga taŋ purāpupul.

2. sakweḥ niŋ gṛha nora tanpa çaka mokirukiran apněd/ winarṇnana,
mwaŋ tekaŋ batur açmawiṣṭaka miraḥ wintuwtu pinik/ rinūpakā,
ñjraḥ tekaŋ wijiliŋ kulāla pinakottamani hatěp ikaŋ gṛhāḍikā,
tañjuŋ keçara cāmpakādinikanaŋ kusuma caracarāñjraḥ hiŋ natār.

Canto 12.

Metre: - - - ᴗ ᴗ - ᴗ - ᴗ ᴗ ᴗ - - - - ᴗ - - ᴗ ᴼ
19 feet, çārdūlawikrīḍita.

1. warṇnan tiṅkah ikaŋ pikaṇděl atathātūt kaṇṭaniŋ nāgara,
wetan/ saŋ dwija çaiwa mukya sira ḍaŋhyaŋ brāḥmarājāḍikā,
ṅkāneŋ dakṣiṇa boḍḍa mukyaṅ anawuŋ saṅkā karṅkannadī,
kulwan/ kṣatriya mantri puṅgawa sa (97a) gotra çrī narendrāḍipa.

2. wetan dan mahl̥t/ l̥buḥ pura narendreŋ wěṅkěr atyādbhutā,
sākṣāt indra lawan saci nṛpati lawan saŋ narendreŋ dahā,
saŋ nātheŋ matahun/ narendra ri lasěm/ muṅgwiŋ dal̥m tan kasaḥ,
kannaḥ dakṣiṇa tan madoḥ kamgětan/ saŋ nātha çobhāhal̥p.

3. ṅkāneŋ ūttara lor sakeŋ pkěn agöŋ kuww ahal̥p/ çobhitā,
saŋ sākṣāt ari de nareçwara ri wěṅkěr saŋ makuww āpagöh,
satyāsiḥ ri narendrādīra nipuṇeŋ nityāpatiḥ riṅ dahā,
kyatiṅ rāt/ maṅaran/ bhaṭāra narapaty āṅde hal̥p niŋ prajā.

4. wetan lor kuwu saŋ gajaḥmada patiḥ riŋ tiktawilwāḍikā,
mantrī wīra wicakṣaṇeŋ naya mataṅwan/ satya bhaktyaprabhū,
wāgmī wāk padu sārjjawopasama dīhotsāha tan lālana,
rāja ḍyakṣa rumakṣa ri sthiti narendrān cakrawarttiŋ jagat.

5. nda ṅkāne kidul iŋ purī kuwu kaḍarmmāḍyakṣan arḍḍāhal̥p,
wetan rakwa kaçaiwan ūttama kaboḍḍākulwan naçryātathā,
tan warṇnan kuwu saŋ sumantry aḍikā len/ mwan saŋ para kṣatriyā,
deniŋ kwehnira bheda ri sakuwukuww āṅde hal̥p niŋ purā.

6. lwir ccandrāruṇa tekanaŋ pura ri tikta çrī(97b)phalanopama,
tejāṅgěh nikanaŋ karaŋ sakuwukuww akweḥ madudwan hal̥p,
lwir ttārāgraha tekanaŋ nāgara çeṣannekha mukyaŋ dahā,
mwaŋ nūṣāntara sarwwa maṇḍalitā rāṣṭrā ṅaçrayākweḥ maṛk.

CHAPTER 3 - TRIBUTARIES.

Canto 13.

Metre: – – – – ᴗ – – ᴗ ᴗ ᴗ ᴗ ᴗ ᴗ – – – ᴗ ᴗ ᴗ ᴥ
20 feet, suwadanā.

1. lwir niŋ nūṣa pranūṣa pramukha sakahawat/ kṣoṇī ri malayu,
   naŋ jāmbi mwaŋ palembaŋ karitaṅ i tĕba len/ ḍarmmāçraya tumūt,
   kaṇḍis kahwas manaṅkabwa ri siyak i ṛkān/ kāmpar mwaṅ i pane,
   kāmpe harw āthawe maṇḍahiliṅ i tumihaŋ parllāk/ mwaṅ i barat.

2. hi lwas lāwan samudra mwaṅ i lamuri batan lāmpuŋ mwaŋ i barus,
   yekāḍinyaŋ watĕk/ bhūmi malayu satanaḥ kapwāmatĕh anūt,
   len tekaŋ nūṣa tañjuŋ nāgara ri kapuhas lawan ri katiṅān,
   sāmpit/ mwaŋ kūṭaliṅga mwaṅ i kūṭawariṅin/ sambas mwaṅ i lawai.

Canto 14.

Metre: ᴗ – ᴗ ᴗ ᴗ – ᴗ – ᴗ ᴗ ᴗ – ᴗ – – ᴗ ᴥ
17 feet, pṛthwī.

1. kaḍaŋḍaṅan i laṇḍa len ri samḍaŋ tiṛm tan kasaḥ,
   ri seḍu buruneŋ ri kalka saluḍuŋ ri solot/ pasir,
   baritw i sawaku muwaḥ ri tabaluŋ ri tuñjuŋ kute,
   lawan ri malano makapramukha ta ri tañjuŋpurī.

2. ikaŋ sakahawan pahaŋ pramukha taŋ hujuŋ medini,
   ri lṅkasukha len ri saimwaṅ i kalantĕn i triṅgano,
   naçor pa- (98a)kamuwar ḍuṅun ri tumasikh/ ri saŋhyaŋ hujuŋ,
   klaŋ kĕḍa jĕre ri kañjap i nirān/ sanuṣa pupul.

3. sawetan ikanaŋ tanaḥ jawa muwaḥ ya warṇnanĕn,
   ri balli makamukya taŋ baḍahulu mwaṅ i lwāgajaḥ,
   gurun makamukha sukun/ ri taliwaŋ ri ḍompo sapi,
   ri saŋhyaṅ api bhīma çeran i hutan kaḍaly āpupul.

4. muwaḥ taṅ i gurun sanūṣa maṅaran ri lombok miraḥ,
lawan tikaṅ i sākṣak ādinīkalun/ kahajyan kabeḥ,
muwaḥ tanah i bāntayan pramukha bāntayan len/ luwuk,
tkeṅ uḍa makatrayāḍinikanaṇ sanūṣāpupul.

5. ikaṇ saka sanūṣanūṣa makhasar butun/ baṅgawī,
kunir ggaliyau mwaṅ i salaya sūmba solot/ muar,
muwaḥ tikhaṅ i waṇḍan ambwan āthawā maloko wwanin,
ri seran i timūr makādiniṅ aṅeka nūṣātutur.

_____

Canto 15.

Metre: ◡ – – – – – – ◡ ◡ ◡ ◡ ◡ – – ◡ ◡ ◡ ◡
17 feet, çikhariṇī.

1. nāhan/ lwir niṇ deçāntara kacaya de çrī narapatī,
tuhun/ taṇ syaṅkāyoḍyapura kimutaṇ ḍarmmānāgarī,
marūtma mwaṇ riṇ rājapura ṅuniweḥ siṅhanagarī,
ri cāmpa kāmbojānyat i yawana mitreka satatā.

2. kunaṇ tekaṇ nūṣa maḍura tatān ilwiṇ parapurī,
ri denyān tuṅgal/ mwaṇ yawaḍāraṇi rakwaikana daṅū,
samudra[1] naṅguṇ[2] bhūmi[3] kta ça- *(98b)* ka kalanya karṅö,
těwěknyan dadyāpāntara sasiki tatwanya tan adoḥ.

3. huwus rabḍaṇ dwīpāntara sumiwi ri çrī narapati,
paḍāsthity awwat/ pāhuḍama wijil aṅkěn/ pratimasa,
sake kotsāhan/ saṇ prabhū ri sakhahaywanyan iniwö,
bhūjaṅga mwaṇ mantrīnutus umahalot/patti satatā.

_____

Canto 16.

Metre: ◡ ◡ ◡ ◡ – ◡ – ◡ ◡ ◡ ◡ – – ◡ ◡ ◡ ◡
17 feet, wilāsinī.

1. krama nika saṇ bhūjaṅgan umareṇ digantara daṅū,
hinilahilān/ swakāryya jaga dona tan swaṅ alahā,
wnaṅ ika yan/ pakon/ nṛpati siṇ parāna ta kunaṇ,
magěhakna çiwagama phalanya tan/panasara.

_____

[1] scribe's note: *4;* [2] id.: *2;* [3] id.: *1.*

2. kunaṅ ika saŋ bhūjaṅga sugatabrateki karṅö,
   apituwin ajña hajya tan asiŋ [1] paranan tikā,
   hinilahila sakulwan ikanaŋ tanaḥ jawa kabeḥ,
   taya riṅ usāna bodḍa mara rakwa sambhawa tinūt.

3. tuhun ikanaŋ digantara sawetaniŋ yawaḍara,
   i gurun i bāli mukya kawnaŋ parānaktikā,
   samāyaniraŋ mahāmuni bharaḍa rakwa mapagĕḥ,
   lawan ikha saŋ munīndra kuturan/ prakāça karṅö.

4. karaṅa ni saŋ bhūjaṅga tinitaḥ ri lakwa rasikha,
   ikaṅ inutus maṅulwana ṅawetanakrama huwus,
   saji saji niŋ lumakwakn i sājña saŋ narapatī,
   sawiku sadā yan āṅujar aweḥ ṛsĕ- (99a) pniṅ umulat.

5. irika taṅ anyabhūmi sakhahĕmban iŋ yawapurī,
   amatĕh i sājña saŋ nṛpati khapwa satya riṅ ulaḥ,
   pituwi siṅ ājñalaṅghyana dinon/ wiçīrṇna sahana,
   tkap ikanaŋ watĕk/ jaladi mantry aneka suyaça.

---

[1] scribe's interpolation : *sa.*

CHAPTER 4 - THE ROYAL PROGRESS.

Canto 17.

Metre: – – – ⏑ ⏑ ⏑ – ⏑ ⏑ ⏑ – ⏑ ⏑ ⏑ ⏑ ⏑ ⏑ – ⏑ ⏑ – ⏑ ⏓
23 feet, jagaddhita.

1. sāmpun/ rabḍa pagĕḥnyadĕg/ nṛpati riŋ yawaḍaraṇi jayeŋ digantara,
ṅkāne çrīphalatiktanāgara sirān/ siniwi mulahakĕn/ jagadḍitā,
kīrṇnaikaŋ yaça kīrtti ḍarmma ginaweniran anukhani budḍiniŋ para,
mantrī wīpra bhūjaṅga saŋ sama wineḥ wibhawa tumut akīrtti riŋ
[jagat.

2. göŋ niŋ wīryya wibhūti kagraha tkap/ nṛpati tuhutuhūttama prabhū,
līlā nora kasaṅçayāniran anamtami sukha sakaharṣaniŋ manaḥ,
kānyā siŋ rahajöŋ ri jaṅgala lawan/ ri khaḍiri pinilih sasambhawa,
astām taŋ kahañaŋ sakeŋ parapurā siṅ aṛja winawe daḷm purī.

3. salwāniŋ yawabhūmi tulya nagarī sasikhi ri paṅadĕg/ narāḍipā,
mewwiwwaŋ janadeça tulya kuwuniŋ bala maṅiḍĕr i khaṇṭaniŋ purī,
saŋ lwir niŋ paranuṣa tulya nika thāniwiṣaya pinahasukainaris,
lwir ūdyana tikaŋ wanādri sahananya jinajar hira tan panaṅçaya.

4. bāryyan/ māsa ri sāmpuniŋ çiçirikāla sira mahasahas macaŋkrama,
wwantĕn thāny a- (*99b*) ṅaran/ ri sima kidul i jalagiri maṅawetan
[iŋ purā,
rāmyāpan/ papunnagyaniŋ jagat i kālaniŋ sawuṅ ika mogha tan pgat,
mwaŋ wewe pikatan/ ri caṇḍi lima lot paraparanira tuṣṭa lālana.

5. yan tan maṅka mareŋ phalaḥ maṛk i jöŋ hyaṅ acalapati bhakti sādara,
pantĕs/ yan panulus ḍatĕŋ ri balitar mwaṅ i jimur i çilāhrit alṅöŋ,
mukyaŋ polaman iŋ dahe kuwu ri liṅgamarabaṅun ika lanenusī,
yan/ riŋ jaṅgala lot sabhā nṛpati riŋ surabhaya manulus mare
[buwun.

6. riṅ çākākṣatisūryya saŋ prabhū mahas/ ri pajaṅ iniriṅ iŋ sanāgara,
   riŋ çākāṅganagaryyamā sira mare lasĕm ahawan i tīraniŋ pasir,
   ri dwārādripanendu paḷnĕṅireŋ jaladi kidul atūt wanālaris,
   ṅkāneŋ loḍaya len tĕtör i siḍĕman/ jinajahira laṅönya yenituŋ.

7. ndān/ riŋ çāka çaçaṅka nāga rawi bhadrapaḍamasa ri tāmbwaṅiŋ
                                                        [wulan,
   saŋ çrī rājasanāgarān mahasahas/ ri lamajaṅ aṅ ituŋ sakhendriyan,
   sakweh çrī yawarāja sapriya muwaḥ tumut i haji sabhṛtyawāhana,
   mantrī taṇḍa sawilwatikta ṅuniweḥ wiku haji kawirājya maŋdulur.

8. ṅkān tekiŋ maparab/ prapañca tumut aŋ- (100a) ḷṅĕṅ aṅiriṅ i jöŋ
                                                        [nareçwara,
   tan len/ saṅ kawi putra saṅ kawi samenaka dinulur anānmateŋ maṅö,
   ḍarmmādyakṣa khasogatan/ sira tkap/ narapati sumiliḥ ri saŋ yayaḥ,
   sakweḥ saŋ wiku bodḍa maŋjuru padāṅatuturakhĕn ulahnireŋ daṅū.

9. ndān tiṅkaḥ rakhawīn maṛk/ ri haji dug/ raray atutur açewa tan
                                                        [salaḥ,
   pinriḥnye hati rakwa milwa saparā narapatin amalar kasanmatā,
   ṅhiŋ tapwan/ wruh apet laṅö pisaniṅun/ tĕtĕsa maminta gīta riŋ
                                                        [karas,
   nā hetunya kamārṇna deça sakamarggā ṅaranika riniñci tūt hawan.

10. tāmbeniŋ kahawan/ winārṇna ri japan/ kuṭi kuṭi hana caṇḍi sāk
                                                        [ṛbaḥ,
    wetan taŋ tĕbu pāṇḍawan ri daluwaŋ babala muwaḥ hi kañci tan
                                                        [madoḥ,
    len tekaŋ kuṭi rātnapaṅkaja muwaḥ kuṭi haji kūṭi paṅkajādulur,
    pañjrak maṇḍala len/ ri poṅgiṅ i jiṅan/ kuwu haṅār i samipaniṅ
                                                        [hawan.

11. prāpteŋ ḍarmma riŋ pañcaçāra tumuluy/ ḍatṅ i kapuluṅān sirāmgil,
    ndān lampaḥ rakawin/ lumāryyāmgil iŋ waru ri hĕriṅ i tira tan
                                                        [madoḥ,
    aṅgāṅgĕḥnya tkap/ bhaṭāra kuṭi riŋ suraya pagĕḥ mara cinārccakĕn,
    ṅhiŋ rakwan kaslaŋ (100b) turuŋ mulih amogha matutur
                                                        [atisāmbhrameŋ maṅö.

Canto 18.

Metre: - - - - ◡ - - ◡ ◡ ◡ ◡ ◡ - - ◡ - - - ◡ - ∘
21 feet, sragdharā.

1. yyankat/ çrī nātha saken̩ kapuluṅan ikanan̩ rājabhr̥tya ṅirin̩ sök,
   salwānin̩ rājamārggāparimita hibkan/ syandanomwat matāmbak,
   wwan̩ nin̩ wwan̩ pekhanin̩ peka tka saha padātī har̩p/ mwan̩ ri
                        [wuntat,
   dūdwan̩ wadwā ḍarāt/ sëḥ girimisën amëḍëp/ mwan̩ gajāçwādi
                        [kīrṇna.

2. nistanyāçaṅkya tan̩ syāndana mapawilaṅan deni cihnanya bheda,
   tëkwan lāmpaḥ nikāpaṇṭa tulis īka dudū ri san̩ mantrī samantri,
   rakryan san̩ mantrī mukyāpatih i majhapahit/ san̩ praṇaleṅ
                        [kaḍatwan,
   pintën/ māwan çata syandana pulupulutan teki cihnanya nekā.

3. san̩ çrī nāthen̩ pajan̩ kweḥni rathanira paḍācihnanin̩ diwaça çrī,
   ndān/ çrī nāthen̩ lasëm/ sök/ rathanira matulis/ nandaka çweta
                        [çobha,
   san̩ çrī nāthen̩ daha cihna sadahākusuma syandanābhrātulis mās,
   mukyan̩ çrī jīwanendrāsakaṭa samasama cihna lobhen̩ ḷwiḥ sök.

4. ndan san̩ çrī tiktawilwaprabhū sakaṭanirāçaṅkya cihnanya wilwā,
   griṅsin̩ lobhen̩ ḷwiḥ lāka paḍa tinulis in̩ mās kajan̩nyān rinëṅgā,
   salwirnin̩ puṅgawāmwat/ bini haji ṅuniweḥ .. çwarī çrī sudewī,
   (101a) sakwehnin̩ pekabhāryyā sakaṭa nika sinan̩ paṅhar̩pnin̩
                        [sapaṇṭa.

5. muṅgwin̩ wuntat/ ratha çrī nr̥pati rinacanan̩ swarṇna rātna pradīpta,
   anyāt/ lwirnyātawin̩ jampana sagala mawālwāhulap/ söṇnya lumra,
   kirṇnen̩ wadwā ṅirin̩ jaṅgala kaḍiri sḍaḥ pan̩laran̩ sök marampak,
   āstam tekan̩ bhayan̩kāryyamawamawa dudūn̩ bhr̥tya muṅgwin̩
                        [gajāçwa.

6. ndaḥ prāpteŋ pañjuran/ muṅkur atiki lariniŋ syandaneñjiŋ
[marāryyan,
lampahniŋ khawy animpaṅ sumĕpĕr i sawuṅān/ maṅlawad/
[wanḍuwarggā,
liṅsirniŋ sūryya maṅkat marṇi ri haliwat/ çrī narendrān lumampaḥ,
tūt mārggāmūrwwa çīghrān ḍatṅ ī watukiken/ ri matañjuŋ
[marāryyan.

7. deçāsimpar kkaboḍḍan kapark i tpiniŋ mārggākaywanya poryyaŋ,
pratyekanye galaṅgaŋ muwah ikaṅ i baḍuŋ tan madoḥ mwaŋ
[baruŋbuŋ,
tan kāryyāṅer mmaṇik/ towi kawiçaya ri yānatrayāṅgĕhnya menöt,
saŋ ḍarmmādyakṣa çīghran/ sinĕgĕhan ika riŋ bhojanāpāna tuṣṭā.

8. sāmpun/ prāpte kulur mwaŋ bataṅ i gaṅan asĕm/ teki lampaḥ
[narendrā,
tistis/ hyaŋ sūryya pintĕn/ ghaṭita pitu siṛm kāmukhan saṅhub
[awrā,
skanḍāwāre tṅaḥ niŋ harahara dinunuŋ çrī narendre kamantyan,
prāptāṅ wyāpāra (101b) sāmpun/ panaḍahira madum/ sthāna tekiŋ
[wwaṅ akweḥ.

___

Canto 19.

Metre: – – – ‿ ‿ – ‿ – ‿ ‿ ‿ – ‿ ‿ ‿ ‿ ‿ ‿ – ‿ – ‿ ๏
23 feet, jagaddhita.

1. eñjiŋ ryyaṅkatiraŋ narendrā ḍatṅ aṅhinĕp i bhayalaṅö tigaŋ kuḷm,
saḥ saṅkerika taŋ kĕdu dawa rame janapada kahalintaṅan huwus,
riŋ lampĕs/ ri timĕs muwaḥ kuṭi ri pogara kahnū ḷbuḥ nika gnĕt,
mwaŋ riŋ maṇḍala hambulu traya tke ḍaḍap adulur ikaŋ rawālaris.

2. wwantĕn/ ḍarmmā kasogatan/ prakāçite madakaripura kastaweŋ
[laṅö,
sīmānugraha bhūpatī saṅ apatiḥ gajamada racaṇanyan ūttama,
yekānuŋ dinunuŋ nareçwara pasaṅgrahanira pinĕnĕd rinūpakā,
andondok mahawan/ rikaŋ trasuṅay andyus i capahan
[atīrthaçewana.

___

2

Canto 20.

Metre: - - - ◡ ◡ - ◡ - ◡ - ◡ ◡ - - - - - ◡ - - - ◡ ⊕
19 feet, çārdūlawikrīḍita.

1. prāptaŋ deça kasogatan/ sahana mawwat bhakta pāne hajī,
   pratyekanya gapuk sadewi çiṣayeṅ içānabajrāpagĕḥ,
   gantĕn poḥ capahan kalampitan iŋ lumbaŋ len/ kuran we ptaŋ,
   mwaŋ pañcar prasamāñça niŋ kuṭi muṅguḥ kapwa tāçraŋ mamaṛk.

2. milwaŋ deça ri tuṅgilis pabayĕman/ rowaŋnya nekāpupul,
   rehnyāṅçe kuṭi rātnapaṅkaja hane caccan kabhūktyāpatĕḥ,
   nāhan ta pabalas/ kasogatan an aṅçāṅgĕḥnya kuww āpagĕḥ,
   bhūkti- *(102a)* nyan pan akāryya kawwalu huwus tiṅkaḥnya ṅūnī
   [daṅū.

Canto 21.

Metre: ◡ - - - - - - ◡ ◡ ◡ ◡ ◡ - - - ◡ ◡ ◡ ⊕
17 feet, çikhariṇī.

1. byatīteñjiŋ maṅkat/ caritan ikanaŋ deça kawahan,
   riŋ lo paṇḍak raṇwakuniŋ i baleraḥ barubare,
   ḍawöhan lāwan kapayĕman i tĕlpak/ ri baṛmi,
   sapāṅ kaprāptan/ mwaŋ kasaduran anujwiŋ pawijuṅan.

2. juraŋ bobo runtiŋ mwaṅ i pasawahan teki kahnū,
   muwaḥ prāpteŋ jalādi patalap ika mwaŋ ri paḍalī,
   riṅ ārṇnon lawan paṅulan i payaman/ len tĕpasana,
   tkeŋ ṛmbaŋ prāpte kamirahan i piṅgir niṅ udadi.

Canto 22.

Metre: ◡ - ◡ ◡ ◡ - ◡ - ◡ ◡ ◡ - ◡ ◡ ◡ ◡ ◡ - - ◡ ◡ ⊕
23 feet, a kind of wikṛti.

1. i ḍampar i patuñjuṅan/ nṛpati lālana mahawan i tīraniŋ pasir,
   amūrwwa hnu tūt/ hnī ratāratā nika magnĕt timbah iŋ ratha,
   arāṛyyan i samīpaniŋ talaga sĕḥ çarasija tarate paḍa skar,
   jnĕk mihat i posikiŋ makara riŋ wway ahniṅ i daḷmnya waspada.

2. ndatan wicaritan kalaṅwan ikanaṅ raṇu masurawayan lawan tasik,
   riyaṅkatira saḥ ḍataṅ ri wḍi ri guntur asnĕt i samīpaniṅ hawan,
   kasogatan i bajrākāṅça ri talaḍwaja tlas apagĕḥ cinarccakĕn,
   dulurnya ri patuñjuṅan/ kaslaṅ i bala turuṅ umuliḥ mareṅ kuṭi.

3. yatekha hinalintaṅan/ muwah amūrwwa matut alas i tīraniṅ pasir,
   (102b) arāryyan irikaṅ palumbwan aburu kṣaṇa lumaris i liṅsiriṅ
                                                                  [rawi,
   bhawiṣya hilintaṅiṅ lwah i rabut/ lawaṅ anuju surud niṅ ampuhan,
   luraḥ ri balater/ linakwanira lālana mamĕgil i tīraniṅ pasir.

4. riṅ eñjiṅ ahawan kunir basini sākṣaṇa ḍatṅ i saḍeṅ sirāmgil,
   piraṅ wṅi kunĕṅ lawasnira jnĕk/ mamṅamṅ i sarampwan aṅlṅöṅ,
   ri saḥnira wawaṅ tke kuṭa bacok/ narapatin awilāça riṅ pasir,
   jnĕk lumihat iṅ karaṅ kinasut iṅ ryyak asirasirat aṅhirib/ jawuḥ.

5. Tuhun rakhawi tan mare kuṭa bacok/ dumadak anut i simpaṅiṅ
                                                                  [hawan,
   aṅūttara sake saḍeṅ mahawan iṅ baluṅ anuju ri tūmbu len habĕt,
   muwaḥ ri galagaḥ ri tanpahiṅ aṅāntya mgil i ṛnĕs apty anaṅkilā,
   amoghā kapapag/ narendrā mahawan/ jayakṛta ri wanagriyālaris.

_____

Canto 23.

Metre: ᴗ – ᴗ – – – ᴗ ᴗ – ᴗ – ᴗ ᴗ
12 feet, waṃçasthā.

1. ri ḍoni bĕṇṭoṅ puruhan lawan bacĕk,
   pakhis haji mwaṅ paḍaṅan/ scaṅ,
   ri jāti gumlar kkawahān çilā bhaṅo,
   aṅūttareṅ dewarame tke ḍukun.

2. muwaḥ lumāmpaḥ ḍatṅiṅ pakāmbaṅan,
   rikā mgil/ saṅ prabhū sākṣaṇān laku,
   ḍataṅ taṅsil/ wwitaniṅ luraḥ ḍaya,
   linakwan aglis/ ḍatṅiṅ juraṅ ḍalm.

3. ikaŋ wahan dug mañalor sakeŋ tasik,
ri sandĕṅ andĕ nikha durggā- *(103a)* mā rupök,
lumud jawuḥ sĕngkanikān paḍālyö,
aneka taŋ syāndana sak/ siliḥ pagut.

Canto 24.

Metre: ◡ – – – – – ◡ ◡ ◡ ◡ ◡ – – ◡ ◡ ◡ ◐
17 feet, çikhariṇī.

1. tuhun maglis/ dug/ ri palayaṅan awarṇnālayaṅ adoḥ,
ri bāŋkoŋ koñaŋ taŋ parana mamgil/ çīghra lumaris,
paḍāmriḥ prāpta riŋ çaraṇa tikanaŋ wwaŋ maçaraṇa,
waneḥ çīghra prāpteŋ surabhaṣarabādniŋ wwaṅ aṅiriŋ.

2. siṛpniŋ ṅwai mandālaṅalaṅ i tkānyeṅ alaṅalaŋ,
ri caṇḍyān dĕgnyaṇḍĕl/ sapi nika waneḥ puḥ bĕsur aṅel,
bhawīṣyāŋ yānā ṅūttara turayan aṅ deça kahawan,
paḍāçrwāṅkatnyāgyātakitāki tkā ri patukaṅan.

Canto 25.

Metre: – – – ◡ ◡ – ◡ – ◡ ◡ ◡ – – – – ◡ – – ◡ ◐
19 feet, çārdūlawikrīḍita.

1. taṅeḥ yan caritan/ pratiṅkah ikanaŋ swabhṛtya mantry adulur,
warṇnan teki ḍataŋnire patukaṅan/ saŋ çrī narendrāpuphul,
ṅkāneŋ sāgaratīra kulwan ikanaŋ tālākṛp alwāratā,
lor parṇnaḥnya sakeŋ pakuwwan irikāṅwan/ çrī narendrāmgil.

2. sakweḥ saŋ para mantry amañcanāgaromuṅwiŋ pakuwwan kabeḥ,
mwaŋ saŋ ḍyakṣa pasaṅguhān/ rasika saŋ waṅçāḍirājomaṛk,
tansaḥ saṅ hupapatty anindita ḍaṅ āçcāryyottarānopama,
çaiwāpañji mapāñji sāntara widagḍeṅ āgama wruḥ kawī.

Canto 26.

Metre: – – – ᵕ ᵕ – – ᵕ – ᵕ ᵕ – – – – ᵕ – – ᵕ – ᵒ
20 feet, a kind of kṛti.

1. ndān mūkya ḍipatīn pakuwwan apagöh saṅ āryya çūrāḍikāra,
    sakweḥ niŋ jajahan/ sa *(103b)* ke patukañan/ sāmpun ḍataŋ tan
    [masowe,
    kapwāsraŋ mahaturhatur paḍā sinūñan wastra buḍḍinya tuṣṭā,
    tuṣṭanyāñdani tuṣṭa ri nṛpati santuṣṭan/ jnĕk/ riŋ pakuwwan.

2. wwantĕn/ rūpaka laryyalaryyan añaḥ saṅke hujuŋnin samudra,
    waiçmāneka kikis tinap natar ikālwāpiṇḍa nūṣan/ sakeŋ doḥ,
    mārggānyeki linantaran/ lyĕp awarṇnaṅguŋ katon denikaŋ ryyak,
    kīrtti saṅ āryya towi pasnāhe prāptya saŋ çrī narendrā.

Canto 27.

Metre: – – – ᵕ ᵕ – – ᵕ – ᵕ ᵕ – – ᵕ – ᵕ ᵕ ᵕ ᵒ
18 feet, a kind of dhṛti.

1. ṅkā çrī nātha marāñlipur huyaṅ i tikṣṇaniŋ dinakara,
    sākṣat dewata dewatin saha khasiḥnirātikaṭikān,
    wwaŋ ri jro sawañ apsarin wahu sakeŋ wihāya madulur,
    moktaŋ klesa hiḍĕp nika mulat awarṇna tibra kawñan.

2. tan tuṅgal/ tikanaŋ wilāça ginawe narendrākasukhan,
    siŋ wastwāsuña tuṣṭacitta rikanaŋ pradeça winañun,
    baryyan karaktan/ çramaçrama maweḥ jñĕr niñ umulat,
    siṅgiḥ dewa mañiṇḍarat/ juga sirān lumañlañ i jagat.

Canto 28.

Metre: ᵕ ᵕ – ᵕ ᵕ – ᵕ ᵕ ᵕ ᵕ ᵕ ᵒ
13 feet, a kind of atijagatī.

1. pira teki lawasnira ri patukañan,
    para mantri ri bāli ri maḍura ḍataŋ,
    ri balumbuñ andĕlan ika karuhun,
    sayawakṣithi wetan umaṛk apuphul.

2. paḍa bhakty ahatur paḍa masirasi(*104a*)ran,
bawi meṣa kbo sapi hayam asu sĕk,
saha wāstra pinuṇḍut adulur/ hasusun,
manahiŋ mulat adbhuta kadi tan i rāt.

3. sakatĕmbay iṅ eñjaṅ atiki caritan,
naranātha sirādadar i bala kabeḥ,
milu salwir ikaŋ para khawi sinuṅān,
paḍa tuṣṭa ti para jana maṅaḷm.

Canto 29.

Metre: – – – ᴗ ᴗ – – ᴗ – ᴗ ᴗ ᴗ – ᴗ ᴗ ᴗ ᴗ ᴗ ᴗ ᵒ
19 feet, kind of atidhṛti.

1. ndan saŋ kawy aparab/ prapañca juga çokha tanari siwuhön,
de saŋ kawy upapatti sogata mapañji kṛtayaça pjaḥ,
mitrāṅgĕh rasike kalaṅwan asih aŋdulur atakitaki,
lagyāmulyani kīrtti pustaka tinumbas inapi tinṅöt.

2. cittaṅkwi rasikan katmwawarasāṅatĕramahasahās,
nyāma wruḥ ri parānaniŋ mahas akīrttya tilara kakawin,
ṅūnīn mātya jmaḥ muwaḥ sisip ikiŋ lara pinahalalu,
mātī pwā ḍatṅiṅhulun/ ḷwĕs aweḥ skĕl analahasā.

3. nāhan kāraṇaniŋ wawaŋ sah umareŋ kṭa milu rumuhun,
tal tuṅgal halalaŋ dawā ri pacaron/ kahawan i buṅatan,
prāpteŋ toya ruṅun/ walaṇḍiṅanujwī tarapas amgil,
eñjiŋ lāryy ahawan/ lmaḥ baṅ irikaŋ kṣaṇa ḍatṅ i kṭā.

Canto 30.

Metre: – – – – ᴗ ᴗ ᴗ ᴗ ᴗ – – – ᴗ – – ᴗ – ᵒ
17 feet, *mandrākrāntā.*

1. rintar saŋ çrī narapati n aṅulwan/ muwaḥ teki warṇnan,
çīghra prāpteŋ kṭa pili- (*104b*) piliḥ pañca rātrin paṅantī,
sweccāmarṇna jalaniḍi n amaṅgiḥ muwaḥ laryyalaryyan,
ndātan dady ālupa riṅ anukhāne parāpan ginöŋ twas.

2. kwehniŋ mantri kṭa paḍā maṛk nāyya mājñā saṅ āryya,
   wīrāpraṇāḍinikha milu saçewa boḍḍopapatti,
   mwaŋ sakweḥ niŋ jajahan aṅiriŋ sök/ ḍataŋ tan hinunḍaŋ,
   kapwāwwat/ bhojana sahana tuṣṭān/ sinūṅan/ suwastra.

Canto 31.

Metre: ᴗ − ᴗ ᴗ ᴗ − ᴗ − ᴗ ᴗ ᴗ − ᴗ − − ᴗ ᴥ
17 feet, pṛthwī.

1. ri saḥnira sakeŋ kṭa mĕwĕh ikaŋ swabhṛtyāṅiriŋ,
   bañu hniṅ ikanaŋ hawan/ wki ḍataŋ ri sampora sök,
   muwaḥ ri daḷman/ tke wawaru riŋ binor hop/ glisan,
   gbaṅ kṛp i glam/ tke kalayu rājakāryyeniwö.

2. ikaŋ kalayu ḍarmma sīma sugatapratiṣṭāpagöḥ,
   mahottama sujanma wanḍu haji saŋ ḍinarmmeŋ daṅū,
   nimittan i pakāryya kāryya haji ḍarmmakāryyaḍikā,
   prasidda mamgat sigīka wkas i suḍarmmenulaḥ.

3. ikaŋ wiḍi wiḍāna sakrama tlas/ gnĕp sāṅkĕpan,
   makādyaṅ upabhoga bhojana haḷp nikānopama,
   amātyagaṇa sāmyasaṅghya çagiri ḍataŋ riŋ sabhā,
   mṛḍaṅga paḍahātri megĕliglan mahiṅan dinā.

4. narendrā ri huwusni kāryyanira seṣṭāni twas ginöŋ,
   asiŋ sakapaṛk/ (105a) pradeça pinaran ḍanondok ḍatĕŋ,
   piraŋ wṅi lawasnirerika parārttha maṅgöŋ sukha,
   surūpa bini hajy uliḥnira wiçeṣa kānyānulus.

5. ri saḥnira sakeŋ kalayw i kutugan kahĕnwālaris,
   ri khĕbwan agĕṅ aglis eṅgal amgil/ ri kāmbaŋ rawī,
   suḍarmma sugatapratiṣṭa racananya çobhah haḷp,
   anūgraha nareçwarā saṅ apatih pu nālāḍikā.

6. haturhatur i saŋ patiḥ ḷwu haḷpnikāninditā,
   byatīta panaḍah narendrā rikanaŋ prabhātocapĕn,
   umaṅkat ahawan/ ri halsĕs i ba ¹ raŋ ri pātuñjuṅan,
   anūntĕn i patĕntĕnan tarub i lesan asrwālaris.

---

¹ erroneous akṣara *roŋ* eliminated by scribe.

Canto 32.

Metre: - - ‿ ‿ ‿ ‿ ‿ ‿ ‿ _ ‿ _ ‿ ‿ ‿ _ ‿ ‿ ‿ ‿ ‿ ⏻
22 feet, a kind of *wikṛti.*

1. çīghrān/ ḍatṅ i pajarakan/ pataŋ dina lawas narapatin amgil,
   ṅkāneŋ harahara kidul iŋ suḍarmma sugatāsana makuwukuwu,
   mantrī wiku haji karuhun saṅ āryya sujanottama paṛṅ umaṛk,
   kapwāṅaturakĕn upabhogha bhojana wineḥ ḍana paḍākasukhan.

2. rīntar narapatin alaris/ wanāçrama ri sāgara ktaṅ usiṛn,
   sĕṅkān/ hawanira maṅidul pakalyan i buluḥ kta kahaliwatan,
   mwaŋ māṅḍala hikaṅ i gḍe samāntara ri sāgara kta kadunuŋ,
   çobhābhinawa ri tṅah i wa- (105b) nāçri racananyan amulaṅunakĕn.

3. ndātan pijĕr umaṛk i jön narendrā rakawin/ jnĕk aṅapi lanö,
   laṅlaŋ lalīta lali laleda lulwi lala menĕh akalis iṅ ulaḥ,
   tamtām/ tan atutur i tutur nikan tut i tatāni saṅ atakitakī,
   jañjān/ jumalajah i jajar ni bañjar ikanaŋ yaça cinaracarā.

4. prāpteŋ pathani ri tpiniŋ tpas/ tpus ikā tpuṅ atĕtĕl atöb,
   seccā macamaca cacahanyan aṅracana bhāṣaracana kakawin,
   kweḥniŋ yaça paḍa dinunam/ wilāpa dadakan/ saha parāb inamĕr,
   pañcakṣara ri wkasan iŋ pralāpa sinamarsamār awtu laṅö.

5. bwat/ rāntĕn atulis atulis kathā patiga watw inasaban aruhur,
   jraḥ nāgakusuma kusumanya riŋ natar i tīra nikha pinarigi,
   andwaŋ karawira kayumās mnūr/ ccaracaranya saha kayu puriŋ,
   mwaŋ nyū gaḍiṅ akuniṅ ahaṅḍap ahwaḥ i padunyan amuhara laṅö.

6. tan ṅeḥ yadi caritan ikaŋ wānāçrama laṅönyan asmu siluman,
   tiṅkaḥnika ri ḍalm i heŋ mahogra tkap iŋ yaça paḍā hinĕduk,
   mwaŋ kweḥ parakaki ṅuniweḥ pareṇḍaṅ atuhāraray ahayu wagĕd,
   moktaŋ mala kaluṣa mihat baṅun/ wihikan iŋ çīwapada sakala.

Canto 33.

Metre: ⏑ ⏑ ⏑ ⏑ – ⏑ – ⏑ ⏑ ⏑ – ⏑ ⏑ – ⏑ ⏑ ⏓
17 feet, narkuṭaka, rajanī.

1. (*106a*) nṛpati mahās/ riṅ açrama wawaŋ sinĕgĕḥ sgĕhan,
tkapira saŋ mahārṣi mapaliṅgih açabda ṛsĕp,
asuṅ upabhoga salwir i bhinuktinire patapan,
nṛpati maḷs/ yathākrama riṅ arttha ḷwĕs kasukhan.

2. paṅucapucapnirān/ gumuṇita rasaniŋ kawikun,
paḍa mawaraḥ ri sesini manaḥnira tan rinṅöt,
wkasan acaṅkrama ḷṅĕṅ asiŋ kalaṅön pinaran,
muhara ri tuṣṭa saŋ tapatapin/ lumihat kawṅān.

3. ri huwusirāŋḷṅön majar i saŋ sutapān muliha,
ri wijilirālaris/ hlahla lumihat kawkas,
tapitapi siŋ rarānwam ahajöŋ paḍākāryy aṅaraŋ,
smara manurun mamañcana sireki hiḍĕpnyan akū.

Canto 34.

Metre: – – ⏑ – ⏑ ⏑ ⏑ – ⏑ ⏑ – ⏑ – ⏓
14 feet, wasantatilakā.

1. yyantuk narendrā kari sūkṣaṅ açramorūk,
priŋnyā kuçābĕh abalut/ ri matālupā ken,
aṅgöŋ taṅis/ sĕṛh ikāyam alas nikājrit,
aluḥ tusiŋ tal aṅaḷḥ syu [1] ṅ ikān pasāmbat.

2. asṛt lari nṛpatin aglis apan tumāmpa,
kweḥniŋ yaçāṛja kamārggā tlas kalalwan,
çīghrān ḍataŋ sira riṅ āryya sarātry aṅanti,
eñjiŋ maṅuttara bhawiṣya ḍataŋ ri gĕṇḍiŋ.

3. saŋ mantry amañcanāgarī karuhun/ saṅ āryya,
siṅhāḍikāra ṅuniweḥ parā çaiwa boddḍa,
kapwā hatūr ttaḍah anindita sopacāra,
(*106b*) mās/ wastra nāma pamaḷs/ nṛpatin/ suke twas.

---

[1] erroneous akṣara *ki* eliminated by scribe.

4. ardḍālawas/ nṛpati tansah añanti māsa,
solahniren̄ sakuwukuww atikan̄ linolyan,
ryyaṅkātnirān hawan i loḥgaway in̄ sumaṇḍin̄,
boran̄ bañör baṛmi tūt/ hnu ñūny añulwan.

Canto 35.

Metre: ‿ ‿ ‿ ‿ – ‿ – ‿ ‿ ‿ – ‿ – ‿ ‿ ‿ – ‿ – – ‿ ᵒ
22 feet, a kind of ākṛti.

1. tuhun i ḍatön nire pasuruhan manimpañ añidul/ ri kāpāñaṅan,
anuluy atūt ḍamārgga madulur tikan̄ ratha ḍatĕn̄ riṅ andoḥ wawan̄,
muwah i kḍu plukh/ lawan i hambal antya nikan̄ pradeçenitun̄,
jhathiti ri siṅhāsāripura rājaḍarmma dinunun̄ narendrāmgil.

2. kunĕn ika san̄ prapañca kari kulwan in̄ pasuruhan pijĕr lālana,
kuṭi mañaran/ riṇḍarbaru ri bhuḥ pradeçanikanan̄ pradeça hujun̄,
yata pinaran/ tinakwanakĕn añca punpunanikā ri san̄ sthāpakā,
likita tinonakĕn/ rasika supraçāsti winacāmañun/ waspada.

3. ikañ i hĕpit/ yathāswa salbak/ wukirnya wiṣayāñca san̄ hyan̄ kuṭi,
satñah i markkaman/ sawah i baluṅhura sawaḥ muwaḥ rin̄ hujun̄,
rasanikanan̄ praçāsti magawe hyuniñ kawi madoha saṅken̄ purā,
ri taya nikan̄ purākṛttha t-hĕr ddaridra musiran̄ kuṭīṇḍarbaru.

4. karaṇaniñ açru maṅkat i huwusnirā mpu masgĕḥ bhawiṣyan̄
[(*107a*) laris,
maluy i kaçewakan/ ḍatñ i siṅhāsāri matutur manaṅkil/ maṛk,
nṛpati huwus mamuspa ri daḷm/ suḍarmma sakatuṣṭanin̄ twas ginön̄,
hana ni kḍun̄ bhirū ri kaçurāṅgaṇān/ mwañ i burn̄ lañönyenitun̄.

Canto 36.

Metre: ‿ ‿ ‿ ‿ – ‿ – ‿ ‿ ‿ ‿ – ‿ – ‿ ‿ ‿ – ‿ – ‿ ‿ ‿ ᵒ
23 feet, açwalalita.

1. krama çubhakāla sahnira ri siṅhāsāri maṅidul mare kagnĕñan,
humaturakĕn kabhaktin i bhaṭāra ḍarmma sawatĕk/ watĕknira tumūt,
ḍana paribhoga bhojana dulurni puspanira sopacara mahaḷp,
saha wasanāwawan/ watañ apaṅruhun paḍaha garjjitan̄ ñwañ umulat.

2. ri huwusirān pañarccana mijil/ ri heŋ pinupul iŋ balākrama maṛk,
para wiku çai sogata saṅ āryya nāligih iniriŋ nirekhi tān adoḥ,
awicaritan/ sḍeŋni panaḍaḥ narendrā tumkāni seṣṭa ri hatī,
bala haji siŋ sasāmbhawa wineḥ suwastra magawe ṛsĕpniŋ umulat.

Canto 37.

Metre: - - ᴗ - ᴗ ᴗ ᴗ - ᴗ - ᴗ ᴗ ᴗ - ᴗ - ᴗ ᴗ ᴗ ᴖ
20 feet, a kind of kṛti.

1. warṇnan/ pratiṅkah ikanaŋ suḍarmma racananya tanpasiriṅan,
dwārātiçobhiten saha mekale yawa ruhurnikāparimitā,
rī jro natar nikā tinumpatumpa tinatāŋ yaçar/jja ri tpi,
sök sarwwa puspa bakulārjja nāhi kusumādya warṇna (107b)
[siluman.

2. prāsāḍa muṅgwī tñah asmū kādbhuta halp nikā hyaṅ aruhur,
lwir meru parwwata çiwapratiṣṭa çiwawimbha muṅgu ri daḷm,
sotan/ bhaṭāra girināthaputra pinakeṣṭi dewa sakala,
aṅgĕḥnirān tuhatuhā narendrā khinabhaktyan i sabhūwana.

3. wwantĕn/ kteka kidul iŋ suḍarmma ri daḷm/ pratiṣṭa katilar,
naŋ bhāpra gopura paḍāruhur kkasugatan/ bataŋ nikā daṅū,
rī jronya ḍaṅka turunan baturnya kari pūrwwa kulwan ananā,
ñhiŋ pūrṇna saṅghyarikha len pamūjan atitaḥ batābaṅ aruhur.

4. naŋ lor batur ni turunanya çeṣani lmahnya sāmpun aratā,
jraḥ nāgapuspa tanĕmanya len taṅ i natar mmasmy asalaga,
heŋ niŋ gupuntĕn ikānaŋ pabhaktan aruhur lmahnya katilar,
alwā natārnya dukutĕn/ hnūnya suktĕn hibĕk lumulumut.

5. lwir stry agriṅ aṅranĕhi rāgi moḷm ikanaŋ cawintĕn awnĕs,
morāwra cāmara nikā kusut/ mapusĕk oli lot kapawaṇan,
nyū danta lāgi lulurĕn/ tapas nikā pucanya tan kram asamun,
moghālume sah i tapiḥnya taŋ çara gaḍiŋ tan āryyakusikan.

6. aṅrs twasiŋ mihat i reḥ nikān taya makoṣaḍā- (108a) nya kawnaṅa,
    ṅhiṅ çrī hayamwuruk inanti he [1] twa ni tuwuḥnya jīwana muwaḥ,
    āpan sirāmupus i kottaman/ tama riṅ ūttamānukani rāt,
    māsiḥ riṅ ātpada lanāwlas i manĕmu duḥkha dewa sakala.

7. warṇnan/ muwaḥ lari nareçwareñjiṅ umareŋ suḍarmma ri kiḍal,
    sāmpun manāmya ri bhatāra liṅsir anuluy/ ḍataŋ ri jajaghu,
    sāmpun muwaḥ maṛk i saŋhyaṅ arcca jinawimbha sontĕn amgil,
    eñjiŋ maluy/ musir i siṅhāsāri tan alḥ marāryyan i buṛŋ.

———

Canto 38.

Metre: - ‿ ‿ ‿ — ‿ — ‿ ‿ ‿ — ‿ ‿ ‿ ‿ ‿ ‿ ℮
17 feet, wamçapatrapatita.

1. rāmya nikā buṛ talaga mumbul ahniṅ abhiru,
    caṇḍi çilā minekala ri maḍya nika rinacanā,
    sök/ yaça muṅgwi piṅgir ikha len/ kuçuma caracara,
    lot paraniŋ macaṅkrama lanāŋjnĕki riṅ umara.

2. tan wuwusĕn laṅö nikā tuhun narapati caritan,
    tistisiṅ ārkka maṅkat ahawan/ tgatgal aruhur,
    rāmya dukut nikātĕtĕl ataṇḍĕs akiris hahijo,
    lwānya sasāgarānak aṅalun juraṅ ikha dinĕlö.

3. çrī naranātha lālana yayā rathanira malaris,
    prāpta ri siṅhāsāri tumame wgilanira huwus,

———

[1] erroneous akṣara *ni* eliminated by scribe.

CHAPTER 5 - KINGS.

Canto 38.

Metre: - ‿ ‿ - ‿ - ‿ ‿ ‿ - ‿ ‿ ‿ ‿ ‿ ‿ ᵒ
17 feet, waṃçapatrapatita.

ndan rakawī ywa mampir i siraŋ sugata muniwara,
sthāpaka rī suḍarmma tuwi go- (*108b*) tra sawala dunun̐ĕn.

4. wṛdḍa halintaṅ i çaçi sahāçra tuwuhira huwus,
sātya suçīla sātkula kaḍaŋ haji suyaça,
pūrṇna tameŋ kriyā mara tan aṅkaḍara panāgara,
kyāti ri mpuṅku hūttama kaṣadpadanira satirūn.

5. çīghra kahāṅçama ywa si wulatnira wawaṅ asgĕḥ,
ḍū lakhi bhāgya saṅ kawi saṅ amrih amaṛk i hajī,
saŋ wnaṅ açrayān masiha ri kadaṅ amlas aṛp,
māsku kadīŋ paṅipyan aparānta pasgĕha tĕmun.

6. ddon/ rakawin parāhyun atañā krama ni tuhatuhā,
çrī naranātha saŋ paḍā dinarmma satata pinaṛk,
mūkya bhaṭāra riŋ kagnĕṅan/ karuhuna wuwusĕn,
pūrwwakathannirān giripatiçwarasuta caritan.

Canto 39.

Metre: ‿ - - - ‿ - - - ‿ - - - ‿ - ᵒ
12 feet, bhujaṃgaprayāta.

1. tuhun/ pādukha mpuṅkwi mun̐guḥ sirojar,
uḍū diwya takwan/ rakawyāñne twas,
mahotsāha siṅgiḥ khawi wṛdḍa buḍḍi,
puriḥ niṅ kaçāstrajan an̐de stutīṅ rāt.

2. nda saŋtabya teki ṅhulun/ mājarosĕn,
maçūcyawway iŋ saptatirtthe çwacittā,
namās te girīndrāya sambaḥ ri saŋhyaŋ,
ndatan dadya kotpāta teki mpaçabda.

3. kṣamā taḥ manaḥ saṅ kawindrān/ rumĕṅwā,
ikaŋ wwaṅ ṛṅö sughyan akweha mityā,
ndan aṅgĕgwa- (*109a*) ne jana saŋ wṛdḍa tekā,
piliḥ nyūnaŋ sughyāḍikā tañ calāna.

Canto 40.

Metre: – – – – ⏑ – – – ⏑ ⏑ ⏑ ⏑ ⏑ ⏑ – – – ⏑ – – ⏑ – ⏑
21 feet, sragdharā.

1. ṅūnī çākābḍi deçendu hana sira mahānātha yudḍekawira,
sākṣat/ dewatmakāyonijatanaya tkap/ çrī girindraprakāça,
kāpwāṛs/ bhakti sakweḥ parājana sumiwī jöŋnirāttwaŋ tumuṅkul,
çrī raṅgāḥ rājasa kyāti ṅaranira jayeŋ çatru çūratidakṣa.

2. deçāgöŋ wetaniŋ pārbwata khawi pnuh iŋ sārwwabhogātirāmya,
kuww aṅgĕḥnyān kamantryan/ maṅaran i kutha rājenadĕḥ wwaŋ [nikā bāp,
yekī ṅgwān/ çrī girīndrātmajan umulahakĕn ḍarmma maṅgöṅ [kaçūran,
tūṣṭāniŋ sāḍu naṣṭāniṅ ahita ya ginöṅ sthityaniṅ rāt/ subhaktī.

3. rī çākābḍī kṛtā çaṅkara sira tumke çrī narendrāŋ kaḍintĕn,
saŋ wīrānindita çrī kṛtajaya nipuṇeŋ çāstra tatwopadeça,
çīghrālaḥ göŋ bhayāmriḥ malajĕṅ anusup ājaran/ pārçwaçūnya,
sakweḥniŋ bhṛtya mukyaŋ para pajurit asiŋ kāri riŋ rājya çīrṇna.

4. ryyālaḥ saŋ çrī narendreŋ kaḍiri girigirīn taŋ sabhūmī jawāṛs,
prāptānĕmbaḥ paḍa wwat/ sahanahana wijil niŋ swadeçān pasewā,
tuṅgal taŋ jaṅgala mwaŋ khaḍiri samasamāṅekanā (*109b*) thātiçantā,
ṅkān tĕmbeniṅ ḍapur mwaŋ kuwu juru tumameŋ sāmya māṅde [sukheṅ rāt.

5. maṅkin/ wṛdḍyāmĕwĕḥ taŋ prabhawa wībhawa riŋ çrī
[girīndrātmasūnu,
enak/ tāndĕl nikaŋ yāwaḍaraṇī sumiwī jöŋ nirān catraniṅ rāt,
rī çākāsyābḍi rudra krama kalahanirān mantuk iŋ swarggaloka,
kyātiṅ rāt/ saŋ dinārmma dwaya ri kagnaṅan/ çҫewaboḍḍeṅ usāna.

Canto 41.

Metre: ᴗ – ᴗ ᴗ ᴗ – ᴗ – ᴗ ᴗ – – ᴗ – ᴗ ᴗ ᴗ – ᴗ – ᴗ ᴗ ᴗ ᴗ
24 feet, a kind of saṃskṛti.

1. bhaṭāra saṅ anūṣanātha wka de bhaṭāra sumiliḥ wiçeṣa siniwī,
   lawasniran amukti riṅ rāt apagĕḥ tikaŋ sayawabhūmi bhakti matutur,
   çākābḍi tilakādri çambhu kalahan/ bhaṭāra mulih iŋ
   [girindrābhawana,
   sireki winaṅun/ praḍipa çimbha çobhita rikaŋ suḍarmma ri kiḍal.

2. bhaṭāra wiṣṇuwarddana kteka putranira saŋ gumanti siniwī,
   bhaṭāra narasiṅhā rowaṅira tulya māḍawa sahāgrajāmagĕh i rāt,
   sirāṅilaṅakĕn/ durātmaka manāma liṅgapati māhi çīrṇṇa sahanā,
   aṛs sahananiŋ paraŋmūkha ri jöŋnireki tuhu dewamūrtti sakalā.

3. i çāka rasa parwwatenduma bhaṭāra wiṣṇwaṅabhiṣeka saŋ suta siwin,
   samāsta parā sāmya riŋ kaḍiri jaṅgalomaṛkh amuspa riŋ purasabhā,
   na- *(110a)* rendra kṛtanāgarekaṅ abhiṣekanāma ri sirān huwus/
   [prakaçitā,
   pradeça kuṭarāja maṅkin atiçobhitāṅaran i siṅhāsāri nāgara.

4. çakābḍa kanawawānikṣithi bhaṭāra wiṣṇu mulih iŋ çūrālaya pjah,
   ḍinarmma ta sire waleri çiwawimbha len/ sugatawimbha muṅgwiŋ
   [jajaghu,
   samāntara muwaḥ bhaṭāra narasiṅhāmūrtti sira mantuk iŋ surāpada,
   hañār sira ḍinarmma de haji ri wĕṅkĕr uttama çiwārcca muṅgwi
   [kumitir.

5. khathākna muwaḥ narendrā kṛtanāgarāṅilaṅakĕn/ kaṭuṅka kujana,
   manāma cayarāja çīrṇṇa rikanaŋ çakābḍa bhūjagoçaçakṣaya pjaḥ,
   nagāsyabhawa çāka saŋ prabhū kumon dumona rikanaŋ tanaḥ ri
   [malayū,
   ḷwĕs mara bhayanya saṅka ri khadewamūrttinira ṅūni kālahan ikā.

Canto 42.

Metre: ⌣ – ⌣ ⌣ ⌣ – ⌣ – ⌣ ⌣ ⌣ – ⌣ ⌣ ⌣ ⌣ ⌣ ⌣ – ⌣ – – ⌣ ๏
23 feet, a kind of wikṛti.

1. çākābḍa yama çūnya sūryya diwaça nṛpati muwah amati durjjana,
ikaŋ mahiṣa raṅkah atyaya kaṭuṅkanikā pinaḷh iŋ sanāgara,
rīṅ aṅgawiyanarkka çāka sira motusan kana ri bāli cūrṇnitan,
ndatan dwa kawnaŋ ratunya kahañaŋ tka i narendrā sakrama.

2. ṣamaṅkana nikaŋ digantara paḍāṅabhaya maṛk i jöŋ nareçwara,
ikaŋ sa- (*110b*) kahawat/ pahaŋ sakahawat malayu paḍā manuṅkul
[ādara,
muwaḥ sakahawat gurun sakahawat/ bakulapura maṅaçrayomaṛk,
ndatan liṅĕn i suṇḍa len/ maḍura pan satanah i yawa bhakti tan
[salaḥ.

3. tuhun/ nṛpati tan/ pramāda luput iŋ mada makin atiyatna riŋ naya,
apan tĕtĕs iŋ kewĕhiŋ bhūwanarākṣaṇa gawayĕn i kālaniŋ kalī,
nimittaniran aŋṛgĕp/ samaya len/ brata mapagĕh apākṣa sogata,
tumīrwa saṅ atītarāja riṅ usāna magĕhakna wṛddiniŋ jagat.

Canto 43.

Metre: – – – ⌣ ⌣ – ⌣ – ⌣ ⌣ ⌣ – – – – ⌣ – – ⌣ ๏
19 feet, çārdūlawikrīḍita.

1. liŋ niŋ çāstra narendra pāṇḍawa rika dwāpāra ṅūni prabhū,
gogendu tri lawan/ çakābḍi diwaçanyāntuknireŋ swaḥpada,
ndaḥ sāntuknira tĕmbayiŋ kali tkaŋ rāt/ mūrkka hārohara,
ṅhiŋ saŋ hyaŋ padabhijña ḍāraka rumakṣaŋ loka dewaprabhū.

2. nāhan hetu narendrā bhakti ri pada çri çakyasiṅhāsthiti,
yatnāgĕgwan i pañcaçila kṛtasaskārābhiṣekākrama,
lumrā nāma jinābhiṣekānira saŋ çrī jñanabajreçwara,
tarkkā wyākaraṇaḍiçāstraṅ inaji çri nātha wijñānulus.

3. ndan/ ri wṛḍḍanireki mātra rumgĕp/ sarwwakriyādyātmikā,
mukyaŋ tantra su- (*111a*) bhuti rakwa tiṅṅöt kempĕn/ rasanye hatī,
pūjā yoga samāḍi pinrihiran amriḥ sthityaniṅ rāt kabeḥ,
āstam/ taŋ gaṇacakra nitya madulu ddann eniwöhiŋ prajā.

4. tan/ wwantĕn karṅö khadi nṛpati sakweḥ sa [1] ṅatīta prabhū,
   pūrṇneṅ ṣadguṇa çāstrawit/ nipuna riṅ tatwopadeçāgama,
   ḍarmmeṣṭāpagĕh iṅ jinābrata mahotsāheṇ prayogakriya,
   nāhan hetuni tusni tusnira paḍaikaccatra dewaprabhū.

5. riṅ çākābḍi jakāryyama nṛpati mantuk/ riṅ jinaindrālaya,
   saṅkai wruḥnira riṅ kriyāntara lawan/ sarwwopadeçāḍikā,
   saṇ mokteṇ çiwabuḍḍaloka talahan/ çrī nātha liṅ niṅ sarāt,
   riṅke sthānanirān ḍinarmma çiwabuḍḍārcca halp/ nottama.

6. lāwan/ riṅ sākgala pratiṣṭā jināwimbhātyānta riṅ çobhitā,
   tkwan nārḍḍanareçwari mwaṅ ika saṇ çrī bajradewy āpupul,
   saṇ rowaṇnira wṛḍḍi riṅ bhūwana tuṅgal/ riṅ kriyā mwaṇ bratā,
   hyaṇ werocana locanā lwiriran ekārcca prakāçeṇ prajā.

- - -

Canto 44.

Metre: - - - - ◡ - - ◡ ◡ ◡ ◡ ◡ - - - ◡ ◡ ◡ ◠
20 feet, suwadanā.

1. tatkāla çrī narendrā kṛtanagara mulih riṅ budḍa bhawana,
   trāsaṇ rāt/ duḥkha hārohara khadi maluyā reḥnyān kaliyuga,
   wwantĕn/ sāma-(*111b*) ntarāja prakaçita jayakatwaṇ nāma kuhakā,
   ṅkāneṇ bhūmī khaḍiryyāpti sumiliha wiçeṣāmriḥ khirakhira.

2. ṅūnī luṅhānira çrī kṛtajaya rikanaṇ çākābḍi manusa,
   ājñā çrī parwwatāḍīndrasuta jayasabhaṅ aṅgantyana siwin,
   riṅ çākāṣṭekanā çāstrajaya muwah umuṅwiṇ bhūmi kaḍiri,
   riṅ çākā trīṇisan/ çaṅkara haji jayakatwaṇ nātha wkasan.

3. sakweḥ niṇ nātha bhakti wkani wka bhaṭārādrīndratanaya,
   āstam/ ri çrī narendra kṛtanagara tkeṇ nuṣāntara manūt,
   maṅke pwe līne saṇ bhūpati haji jayakatwaṅ mūrkka wipathā,
   kewĕḥ niṅ rāt/ rinakṣeṅ kali niyata hayunya tan dadi lanā.

- - -

[1] erroneous akṣara *ti* eliminated by scribe.

4. paṅdānī wruḥnireŋ çāstra paṅawaçani kotsāhan haji daṅū,
moghā wwantěn/ wka çrī nṛpati malahakhěn/ çatrwāmahayu rāt,
ndan māntwāṅgěḥnira dyaḥ wijaya panlah iṅ rāt/ māstawa sira,
ārddā mwaŋ twaŋ tatar mmamṛpi haji jayakatwaŋ bhraṣṭa sahana.

———

Canto 45.

Metre: ᴗ ᴗ – ᴗ ᴗ ᴗ ᴗ – – ᴗ ᴗ ᴗ – ᴗ ᴗ ᴗ ᴗ ᴗ
18 feet, a kind of dhṛti.

1. ri pjaḥ nṛpa jayakatwaṅ awa tikaŋ jagat alīlaŋ,
māsa rūpa rawi çakābḍa rika narāryya sira ratu,
siniwiŋ pura ri majhāpahit/ tanurāga jayaripu,
tinlaḥ nṛpa kṛtarājasa jayawarddana nṛpati.

2. satěwěk nṛpa kṛtarā- *(112a)* jasa jayawarddana siniwī,
sayawākṣithi maluy ātutur atisādaran umaṛk,
paḍa harṣajan umulat/ ri payugala nṛpati catur,
duhitā nṛpa kṛtanāgara paḍa tulya surawaḍu.

———

Canto 46.

Metre: – – – ᴗ ᴗ – ᴗ ᴗ – ᴗ ᴗ ᴗ – – – ᴗ – – ᴗ
19 feet, çārdūlawikrīḍita.

1. ndan saŋ çrī parameçwarī tribhuwaṇā namāgrajānindita,
tansaḥ dyaḥ duhitā prakāçita mahādewyānulus/ riŋ hajöŋ,
prājñā pāramitākya saŋ makajayendrā dewyānindyeŋ raras,
dyaḥ gāyatry anurāga wuṅsu pinakādin/ rājapatnīŋ puri.

2. ndan rakwekin atmwamiṅtiga sirān/ wwaŋ sānak ārddapaṛ,
āpan rakwa bhaṭāra wiṣṇu mamisan/ parṇṇahnirān tan madoḥ,
lāwan/ çrī narasiṅhāmūrtti wka ri dyaḥ ḷmbu tal/ suçrama,
saŋ wīreŋ laga saŋ ḍinarmma ri miṅ boḍḍapratiṣṭāpagöḥ.

———

Canto 47.

Metre: - - ◡ - - ◡ ◡ ◡ - - ◡ ◡ - ◡ - ∘
14 feet, wasantatilakā.

1. dyaḥ ḷmbu tal/ sira maputra ri saŋ narendrā,
   na donnirān ṛsĕp amiŋtiga len suputrī,
   na lwir pawornni pakuṛn haji saikacittā,
   sājñānirājña kinabehan aweḥ sukeṅ rāt.

2. riŋ çāka sapta jana sūryya narendrā warṇnān,
   māstwākĕn ātmajanirān siniwīŋ kaḍintĕn,
   çrīndreçwarībunira wīra widagḍa wijña,
   rājābhīṣeka jayanāgara tan hanoli.

3. riŋ çā- (*112b*) ka mātryaruṇa līnaniraŋ narendrā,
   drāk pīnratiṣṭa ¹ jinawimbha sireŋ purī jro,
   antaḥpurā ywa panlaḥ rikanaŋ suḍarmma,
   çaiwāpratiṣṭa sira teki muwaḥ ri simpiŋ.

Canto 48.

Metre: - ◡ ◡ - ◡ - ◡ ◡ ◡ - ◡ - ◡ ◡ ◡ - ◡ - ◡ ◡ ◡ ∘
22 feet, madraka.

1. ndaḥ kawkas narendrā jayanāgara prabhū ri tiktawilwanāgarī,
   mwaŋ nṛpaputrīkāntĕnira maibu saŋ prawara rājapatny anupama,
   saŋ rwa paḍotameŋ hayu baṅun/ rwaniŋ ratin anorakĕn/ surawaḍu,
   nātha ri jīwanāgrajanira nṛpe daha sira pamuṅsu siniwī.

2. riŋ çakakalla mukti guṇa pākṣa rūpa maḍumāsa tapwa caritān,
   çrī jayanāgara prabhūn umaṅkat aṅhilaṅakĕn musuḥ ri lamajaŋ,
   bhraṣṭa pu namti sāk sakulagotra ri pajarakan/ kuṭanya kapugut,
   wrinwrin aṛs tikaŋ jagat i kaprawiranira saŋ narendrā siniwī.

3. riŋ çakakāla windu çara sūryya saŋ nṛpati mantuk iŋ haripada,
   çīghra sirān ḍinarmma ri daḷm purārccanira wiṣṇuwimbha parama,
   len ri çilā ptak/ mwaṅ i bubāt paḍā pratima wiṣṇumūrtty anupama,
   riŋ sukhalīla taŋ sugatawimbha çobhitan amoghasiddi sakala.

---

¹ erroneous akṣara *ri* eliminated by scribe.

Canto 49.

Metre: ⌣ – – ⌣ – – ⌣ – – ⌣ – ∘
12 feet, bhujaṃgaprayāta.

1. tuhun/ riṅ çākābḍendu bāṇa dwi rūpa,
   nr̥pe jīwāna kyāti mātā narendrā,
   gumantī rīkaṅ tiktamālura rājñi,
   pitā çrī narendrā rikaṅ siṅhāsāri.

2. pa- (*113a*) niṅkaḥnira çrī mahārājapatni,
   sirā teki maṅgālya riṅ rāt wiçeṣā,
   sutā mantu len potrakān/ rāja rajñī,
   sirāṅratwakĕn/ mwaṅ rumākṣeṅ sakāryya.

3. riṅ āgnipwarī çāka taṅ çatru çīrṇna,
   saḍeṅ mwaṅ kṭālaḥ dinon iṅ swabhr̥tya,
   twĕkniṅ jagadrākṣaṇa bwatnya sumraḥ,
   ri saṅ mantryanāmaṅ madatyanta wijñā.

4. muwaḥ riṅ çākabdeṣu māsākṣi nabhbhī,
   ikaṅ bāli nāthanya duççila nīcchā,
   dinon iṅ bala bhraṣṭa sakweḥ nāça,
   ars sālwir i duṣṭa maṅḍoḥ wiçathṭa.

5. ḍaṅ ācāryya ratnāṅça nā liṅnirojar,
   tuhūjar niṅ saṅ wr̥ḍḍa pojarnirāṅras,
   katon kottaman/ çrī narendrerikaṅ rāt,
   apan dewawaṅçāthawā dewamūrtti.

6. ikaṅ wwa rumĕṅwi kathā çrī narendrā,
   nda yan tr̥pti cittanya membuḥ kabhaktin,
   awas pāpakarmmanya maryyāṅaweça,
   ikaṅ duḥkha rogādi mawas wināça.

7. muwaḥ pādukha mpuṅku mopakṣamojar,
   ikiṅ paṅrĕṅö māsku iṅanya maṅkā,
   tumĕmwaṅ hita wr̥ḍḍyani paṇḍitatwā,
   phalāniṅ mucap/ kasthawan saṅ wiçeṣa.

8. huwusniṅ sgĕḥ sakramān arjjawāṅliṅ,
   rakawyāmwitānolihekiṅ swakāryya,
   tkaṅ ratrī sontĕn/ mgil/ ri pakuwwan,
   kṣaṇeñjiṅ manaṅkil ri jöṅ narendra.

———

CHAPTER 6 - THE CHASE.

Canto 50.

Metre: – – – ‿ ‿ ‿ ‿ – ‿ – – ‿ – ᴏ
13 feet, praharṣiṇī.

1. *(113b)* warṇnan/ çrī nṛpati mahās mareŋ paburwan,
maṅkat sāyuḍa saha bhṛtya len/ rathāçwa,
ṅkāneṅ nandakawana kānanātidurgga,
kaywanyādbhutatara kāça muñja kīrṇna.

2. medran taŋ bala balabar huwus manĕṅkö,
lāwan/ syandana madan aṅrapĕt/ raṅköt,
kedran taŋ wana wanaranya kagyat awri,
awṛg/ pakṣinika mapakṣa mūra khegu.

3. hūŋ niŋ bhṛtya mawurahan matunwatunwān,
ghūrṇnāŋwarṇna paçurakiŋ tasik/ gumĕntĕr,
untabnyagni nika dudug riṅ antarāla,
sākṣat kanḍawawana de hyaṅ agni ṅūnī.

4. tonton taŋ mṛga malayū ndatan wri rātnya,
kewran/ wibhrama marbut haṛp marampak,
apan miṅgata balabar kkaṛsnikeṅgī,
etunyākukud umusī tṅah matimbun.

5. kwehnya lwir ggawaya ri gobrajāprameya,
lwir goh riŋ wṛṣabhapurāṅbĕk/ prakīrṇna,
wök sĕṅgah gawaya lulāya çalya cihna,
goḍeya plawaga wiḍāla gaṇḍakāḍi.

6. satwāsiŋ sahana rikeṅ alas/ pralabḍa,
kapwātūt manah ika tan hana wiroḍa,
kadyāhĕm/ pinakajurunya taŋ mṛgendrā,
ṅkāne saṇḍiṅ ika çiwā maṛk tan eṅgī.

Canto 51.

Metre: ◡ — ◡ ◡ ◡ — ◡ — ◡ ◡ ◡ — ◡ — — ◡ ⊖
17 feet, pṛthwī.

1. kṣamākna patakwaniṅ hulun i saŋ mṛgendrādipā,
   gati nṛpatin aṅraraḥ gahana toḥ *(114a)* naya ndyaŋ gĕgĕn,
   aṅantya juga matya riŋ paṅadgan/ malaywā kunĕŋ,
   mwaṅ alagana denya tulya hayuyun/ dinoḥ tan murud.

2. awarṇna kadi maṅkanojar ikanaŋ çṛgālomaṛk,
   ikaŋ hariṇa kṛṣnasāra ruru cihna mojar wwawa,
   yan i bwat i patikta tan hana muwaḥ nayāgĕgön,
   khalena saka riŋ malaywamalarolihaṅ uṅsiṛn.

3. ikaŋ gawaya serabha wṛṣabha len tarakṣāmuwus,
   aḍā wipathā koŋ knas tuhutuhun/ mṛgālpāḍama,
   ndatar lkasaniŋ suḍiraṅ alayū maṅantyā kunaŋ,
   si maṅlawana ḍarmma gĕgwana malar tumĕmwaṅayu.

4. mṛgendra sumawur kaliḥ paḍa wuwusta yuktīyagĕgön,
   nda yan wruha mabhedakhĕn sujana durjjanannūŋ dlĕn,
   yan iŋ kujana wāhya solaha malaywa maṅswā kunaŋ,
   apan wipalaṅ aṅga patyana tkapnya tanpadon.

5. tuhun pwa yan i saŋ tripakṣa ṛsi çaiwa boddā tuwī,
   malaywa jugan enakāṅiriṅane sirān/ paṇḍita,
   kunaṅ pwa kita yat kapaṅgiha tkan narendrāburu,
   aṅantya pati khewalāwwata huripta haywāgigu.

6. apan/ nṛpati yogya paṅhañutane huripwiŋ dadī,
   bhaṭāra giripatyamūrtti ri sirā *(114b)* n/ wiçeṣa prabhū,
   awas hilaṅa pāpaniŋ pjaḥha denirāmatyana,
   lwiḥ saka ri kottamāniṅ alabuḥ ri saŋ hyaŋ raṇu.

7. syapeka musuhakwa ri bhūwana yan paḍe meḍani,
   tathāpi ri sira tripakṣa mariris/ ṅwaṅ andoḥ wawaŋ,
   pitowi haji yan ta katmwa niyatāku kawwat/ hurip,
   ndatan muwaha satwajāti phalaniŋ pjaḥ denira.

Canto 52.

Metre: ⌣ ⌣ – ⌣ ⌣ – ⌣ ⌣ – ⌣ ⌣ ⊖
12 feet, toṭaka.

1. kadi mojara kumwa kitan papupul,
   wkasan parṅ aṅhaḍa yan/ humar̥k,
   bala peka sahāstra kaduk maburu,
   pinagut niṅ açr̥ṅga maluy malayū.

2. tucapa mamawāçwa parṇ maburu,
   tinujunya warāha sḍĕṇ mapupul,
   kasihan karawaṇnyan aneka pjaḥ,
   rinbut saha putra tatan/ pabisā.

3. manalandaṅi teki karūṇnya masö,
   saka pāt lima bhinna magöṇ maruhur,
   ampaḥ ta tutuknya mabāṇ ri mata,
   paḍā rodra sihuṇ nika tulya curik.

4. ikanaṇ çwana mamuk kinarātnya pjaḥ,
   hana rantas iganyaṇ gulūnya pgat,
   rinbut muwah alwaṅi malwaṅ arok,
   papagutnya baṅun laga rodra jmur.

Canto 53.

Metre: ⌣ ⌣ ⌣ ⌣ – ⌣ – ⌣ ⌣ ⌣ – ⌣ – ⌣ ⌣ ⌣ ⊖
17 feet, wilāsinī.

1. tucapaṅ aburwanūt hariṇa mañjaṅan silih uhuḥ,
   sasikhi wināṅswan/ ginayur aṇgayor gĕyuh alon,
   laku nika pan/ kĕ- (115a) noru ruḍira drawādr̥s aṅbĕk,
   duduṅ asakit/ kne pada pināda mawyat anibā.

2. apulih ikaṇ balātri saha tumbak akral aṅusī,
   atunah ikaṇ knas timuta mañjaṅān/ lwaṅ ika bāp,
   apuliha hikaṇ wiṣāna gawayādi satwa magalak,
   bubar alayū bala nr̥pati kagyat alwaṅ iniwud.

3. hana maṅusir juraŋ sukĕt aliṇḍuṅan/ tahĕn agöŋ,
   duduṅ umanek mareŋ paṅ arbut/ ruhur kaburayūt,
   kasihan ikaŋ musir kkayu rumaṅkaraṅkal umaluy,
   kaparpĕkan/ wtisnya winiṣāṇa kagyat akidat.

4. kṣaṇa para māntry aneka saha wāhanāçraṅ apuliḥ,
   amataṅ anūla maŋḍuk anuligy amāṇḍĕm anujaḥ,
   karaṇanikaŋ wiṣabi malayū gṛbĕgnya gumṛḥ,
   tinut inusīnuyālwaṅ ika kīrṇna çīrṇna rinbut.

5. wiku haji çaiwa bodḍa hana milw anumbak aburu,
   ginluran iŋ tarakṣa malajöṅ tinūt maṅudidiŋ,
   lali riṅ upakriya ṅga nika tan suçīla ta kunĕŋ,
   tumut aṅiwö kawāhyan alupān huwus/ kṛtawarā.

Canto 54.

Metre: – – – ◡ ◡ – – ◡ – ◡ ◡ ◡ – – – – ◡ – – ◡ •
19 feet, çārdūlawikrīḍita.

1. warṇnan/ çrī naranātha sāmpun umanek/ riŋ syandananinditā,
   çobhātyanta ruhurnya patya tikanaŋ sapyāmatĕk nirbhaya,
   (115b) muṅsi maḍyanikaŋ wanāntara manūt/ burwan siṅ aṅde takut,
   etunyālaradan/ mgat bala paraṅḍoḥ taŋ çawānyālayū.

2. kāryyaŋ sūkara kṛṣṇaçāra ruru cihnāḍinya maṅgöŋ bhaya,
   tandaŋ çrī nṛpatin/ mawāhana turaṅga nūt/ riyātryālayū,
   māntrī taṇḍa bhūjaṅga kapwa saṅ umūṅgwiṅ açwa milw aburu,
   bhraṣṭaŋ satwa dinūk/ tinumbak inirās kinris pjaḥ tanpagāp.

3. ārdḍālwā maratā lmaḥ tuwin alas/ ṅköd ri sornyāpaḍaŋ,
   etunyaṅ hariṇātidurbbala tinūt/ saglisnya deniŋ kuda,
   tuṣṭāmbĕk/ nṛpatīn parāryyan anaḍaḥ mantrī bhūjaṅgomark,
   mājar solahirān/ pakolih irikaŋ soliḥniraṅde guyu.

CHAPTER 7 - THE RETURN.

Canto 55.

Metre: ⌣ ⌣ ⌣ ⌣ – ⌣ – ⌣ ⌣ ⌣ – ⌣ ⌣ ⌣ ⌣ ⌣ ⌣ – ⌣ – ⌣ ⌣ ⌣ °
24 feet, kind of saṃskṛti.

1. awicaritan gati nṛpati yan/ maburu jnök i rāmyaniṅ giriwana,
   hanan umulih mareṅ kuwukuwū maluy amawa ri saṅ para nṛpawaḍū,
   kadi lariniṅ macaṅkrama hanan kadi tumkani rājyaniṅ ripukulā,
   wruhira ri doṣaniṅ mṛga tatar/ wyasana siran ahiṅsaḍarmma gin-gö.

2. caritan ulahnirān madan umantuka maṅĕn i kalaṅwaniṅ swanāgara,
   krama çubhakāla maṅkat ahawan/ bañu haṅĕt i banir/ mūwaḥ
   [talijuṅān,
   amgil i wḍawaḍwan irikaṅ dina (116a) mahāwan i kūwarāha ri cloṅ,
   mwaṅ i dadamār ggarantaṅ i pagör talagā pahañaṅan/ tkekha
   [dinunuṅ.

3. rahina muwaḥ ri tāmbak i rabut wayuha ri balanak linakwan alaris,
   anuju ri pāṇḍakan/ ri bhaṇarāgin amgil i ḍatĕṅ nire padāmayan,
   maluy aṅidul/ maṅulwan n umare jajawa ri suku saṅ hyaṅ adri
   [kumukus,
   maṛk i bhaṭāra ḍarmma saha puspa paḍa paḍaha garjjita wwaṅ
   [umulat.

Canto 56.

Metre: – – – ⌣ ⌣ – ⌣ – ⌣ ⌣ ⌣ ⌣ – ⌣ – ⌣ ⌣ ⌣ °
18 feet, a kind of dhṛti.

1. ndan tiṅkah nikanaṅ suḍarmma riṅ usāna rakwa kaṛṅö,
   kīrtti çrī kṛtanāgara prabhū yuyut nareçwara sira,
   tĕkwān rakwa sirāṅaḍiṣṭita çarīra tan hana waneḥ,
   etunyaṅ dwaya çaiwa boḍḍa saṅ amūja ṅūni satatā.

2. cihnaŋ caṇḍi ri sor kaçaiwan apucak kaboḍḍan i ruhur,
mwaŋ ri jro çiwawimbha çobhita haḷpnirāparimitā,
akṣobhyapratime ruhur mmakuṭa tan hanolyantikā,
saṅke siḍḍinirān/ wināça tuhu çūnyatatwaparamā.

(Between canto 56 and canto 57 the double pada is missing.)

Canto 57.

Metre: ⌣ ⌣ ⌣ ⌣ ⌣ ⌣ — ⌣ — — ⌣ — — ⌣ — — ⌣ ⚬
18 feet, mahāmālikā.

1. hanā māta karnö tĕpĕk/ saŋ hyaṅ akṣobhyāwimbhan/ hilaŋ,
prakaçita pada pādukha çrī mahāgurwi rājaḍikā,
sutāpa çuci çuçilā boḍḍabrata çrawanāninditā,
anupama bahuçiṣya sāmpun macīryyan mahāpaṇḍitā.

2. sira (116b) ta mahās atīrtha seccāmgil/ riŋ suḍarmma ḍaḷm,
praṇata mark i saŋ hyaṅ arccātibhaktyāṇḍarāṅastutī,
yataṅ amuhara çālyani twasniraŋ sthāpakānaṅçaya,
ri wnaṅanira bhaktya ri hyaŋ çiwārccātañā ṅakṣama.

3. muniwara mawaraḥ sire tatwa saŋ hyaŋ suḍarmmeŋ danū,
mwaṅ i hananira saŋ hyaṅ akṣobhyawimbhātisūkṣme ruhur,
ryyulihiran umaluy/ muwaḥ maṅhinĕp/ riŋ suḍarmmomark,
salahāça kawṅan sirān ton/ ri mukṣa hyaŋ ṅārccālilaŋ.

4. pilih anala çarārkka rakwa çakābde hyaṅ ārccan hilaŋ,
ri hilaṅira sināmbĕr iŋ bajraghoṣa sucaṇḍi daḷm,
pawarawarahiraŋ mahāçrāwakāwas/ ndatan saṅçaya,
pisaniṅu waluya ḍārmma tkwan kadohan huwus.

5. aparimita haḷpni tiṅkaḥ nika swarggatulyānurun,
gupura ri yawa mekala mwaŋ balenyāçaka pwāḍikā,
ri ḍaḷm inupacāra sĕk nagapuspāndĕŋ,
prasama wijah arūmpukan/ çārasaŋ strī daḷm nāgarī.

6. pira kharika lawas narendrān/ sukhācaṅkramāpet laṅö,
ri wulu ḍaḍa tatāka mendaḥ pakisnyāŋjrah i jro bañu,
pinaraniran amūrwwa saṅke suḍarmmāṅkĕn arkkāpanasan,
mwaṅ umara ri pakalwaṅan/ tūt juraŋ (117a) seccaniŋ twas ginöŋ.

Canto 58.

Metre: – ◡ ◡ – ◡ ◡ – ◡ ◡ ◡ – ◡ ◡ – – ◡ ◡ – ◡ ◡ ⌐
20 feet, a kind of kṛti.

1. warṇnan i saḥnira riṅ jajawa riṅ paḍāmeyan ikaṅ dinunuṅ,
   maṇḍĕ cūṅgraṅ apet kalaṅön/ numahās iṅ wanadeçāḷṅöṅ,
   ḍarmma karṣyan i pārçwaniṅ acala pawitra tikaṅ pinarān,
   rāmya nikān pañuṅaṅ luralurah inikhötnira bhāṣa khiduṅ.

2. sāmpunirāṇlñeñ eñjiṅ atihaṅ ikanaṅ ratha sāmpun adan,
   maṅkat aṅulwan i jöṇniṅ acala mahāwan sakhamārgga daṅū,
   prāpty amgil/ ri japān nṛpati pinapag iṅ balasaṅghya ḍataṅ,
   siṅ kari ri pura monĕñ i parkhan ikān paḍa harṣa mark.

3. kāla ḍawuḥ tiga taṅ diwaça ri panaḍaḥ nṛpatīn mapupul,
   mūkya nareçwara rāma haji khalih umuṅwatitaḥ pinark,
   saṅ nṛpatī matahun ri paguhan i hiriṅ nṛpatīn tan adoḥ,
   kāpwa sadāmpati soway i panaḍahirekana tan/ wuwusĕn.

Canto 59.

Metre: ◡ ◡ ◡ ◡ – ◡ – ◡ ◡ ◡ – ◡ ◡ – ◡ ◡ ⌐
17 feet, narkuṭaka, rajanī.

1. narapati maṅkat eñjiṅ awan sakathān lumaris,
   rakhawi lumāryyanimpaṅ i rabut tugu lan/ pañiriṅ,
   sumĕpĕr iṅ pahyaṅan/ katĕmū taṅ kulawanḍwapupul,
   paḍa masgĕḥ mupākṣamaknalpanikān dunuṅön.

2. nṛpati halintaṅ i banasara mwaṅ i saṅkan adoḥ,
   ḍatṅ i pamiṅgir iṅ pura pilih ghaṭita rwa huwus,
   sakahnū sök lĕbuh nika gajāçwa padātyasusun,
   ki- (*117b*) mutaṅ maraṅ kbo gaway apanḍarat ārdḍa pnuḥ.

3. khadi tinitaḥ lari sakrama yan padulur,
   nṛpati pajaṅ saha priya sabhṛtya sirān rumuhun,
   nṛpati ri lasĕm ri wuntatira maṅka ta muwaḥ tan adoḥ,
   rathanira khapwa çobhita maweḥ sukhaniṅ lumihat.

4. narapati ri dahā nṛpati ri wĕṅkĕr umuṅgwi wugat,
nṛpati ri jīwane wuri sabharttṛ sabhṛtya tumūt,
makapamkas/ ratha nṛpati kīrṇna sapaṇta pnūḥ,
piraṅ iwu khapwa sayuḍa tikaṇ bhaṭa mantry aṅiriṇ.

5. tucapa tikaṇ wwaṅ iṇ lbuh atāmbak i tĕmbiṅ atip,
atĕtĕl ayöm aṅanti ri halintaṅa saṇ nṛpatī,
ḍaraḍara taṇ waḍū mtu mareṅ lawaṅ atry aṛbut,
hana kahuwan salāmpur i ghanasnikha yar palayū.

6. ikanaṅ ado gṛhanya maṛbut/ khayukaywaruhur,
makaburayūt ri pāṇ nika rarātuhā manwam atöb,
hana tirisan liraṇ ywa pinaneknika tan panahā,
sahaja lalīn katon/ pijĕr anona jugaṇ kinire.

7. ri ḍatṅiraṇ narendrā̃ kalaçaṅka humuṇ mabaruṇ,
sahana nikaṇ wwaṅ iṇ lbuh umĕṇḍĕk aṛs māraṛm,
ri kahaliwatnirātrik/ tikanaṇ maṅiriṇ riṅ untā- *(118a)* t,
gaja kuda garḍḍabhoṣtra guluṅan/ gumuluṇ tan aṛn.

Canto 60.

Metre: ◡ ◡ ◡ ◡ – ◡ ◡ – ◡ ◡ – ◡
12 feet, abhinawatāmarasa.

1. ikaṅ aḍarat/ bala peka marāmpak,
pipikupikul nika kīrṇna ri wuntat,
mirica kasumba kapas kalapa wwaḥ,
kalar asĕm pinikul saha wijyān.

2. i wuri tikaṇ mamikul abwat,
khapasah arepwan arimbit anuntun,
kirikirik iṇ tṅĕn i kiwa bĕñcit,
pitik itik iṇ kisa mewĕd araṅkik.

3. sasiki pikulpikulanya maghaṇṭaḥ,
khacu kacubuṇ buṅ upiḥ khamal anwām,
tapi kukusan haruḍaṇ ḍulaṅ uswān.
lwir amurutuk/ çaranya ginuywan.

4. nṛpati paṛŋ ḍatṅ i pura warṇnan,
   tlas umuliḥ ri dalmira sowaŋ,
   atutur i solaḥ-hulaḥnira ñūntĕn,
   asiṅ anukāna para swa ginöŋ twas.

(Between canto 60 and canto 61 the double pada is missing.)

CHAPTER 8 - PROGRESSES SOUTH.

Canto 61.

Metre: – – – – ⏑ ⏑ ⏑ ⏑ ⏑ – – – ⏓
13 feet, a kind of atijagatī.

1. luṅhaŋ kāla nṛpati tan alawas riŋ rājya,
prāptaŋ çākha dwi gaja rawi bhadraŋ māsa,
ṅkā ta çrī nātha mara ri tirib/ mwaŋ sömpur,
burwan sasök/ hyalas ika dinwan lwaŋnyākweḥ.

2. ndan ri çakha tri tanu rawi riŋ weçāka,
çrī nātha mūja mara ri palaḥ sabhṛtya,
jambat siŋ rāmya pinaranirān/ lāṅlitya,
ri lwāŋ wĕntār mmaṅuri balitar mwaŋ jimbe.

3. jañjan saṅke (*118b*) balitar aṅidul tūt/ mārgga,
sĕṅkān/ poryyaŋ gatarasa tahĕnyādoḥ wwe,
ndaḥ prāpteŋ loḍaya sira piraŋ rātryāṅher,
çakte rūmniṅ jalaḍi jinajaḥ tūt piṅgir.

4. saḥ saṅke loḍaya sira maṅanti ri simpiŋ,
swecchānambyāmahajöṅa ri saŋ hyaŋ ḍarmma,
sākniŋ prasaṅda tuwi hana doḥnya ṅulwan,
nā hetunyān/ baṅunĕn aṅawetan matra.

Canto 62.

Metre: – – – ⏑ ⏑ – ⏑ – – ⏑ ⏑ ⏑ – – – – ⏑ – – – ⏑ – ⏓
20 feet, a kind of kṛti.

1. mwaŋ tekaŋ parimaṇa tapwa pinatūt wyaktinya lāwan praçāsti,
hetunyān tinapan/ samāpa ḍinĕpan/ pūrwwāḍi sāmpun tinugwan,
ndan saŋ hyaŋ kuṭi riŋ guruŋguruṅ ināmbil/ bhūmya saŋ hyaŋ
[suḍarmma,
gontoŋ wiṣṇu rare kabajraḍaraṇekā paŋhli çrī narendrā.

2. yyāntuk/ çrī narapaty amārgga ri jukuŋ jo yānabajrān/ pamūrwwa, prāpta rāryyan i bajralākṣmin amgil/ ri çūrabhāṇe suḍarmma, eñjiŋ yyāṅkatirān/ parāryyan i bkĕl/ sontĕn ḍatĕŋ riŋ swarājya, sakweḥ saŋ maṅiriŋ muwaḥ tlas umantuk/ riŋ swaweçmanya sowaŋ.

CHAPTER 9 - RĀJAPATNĪ.

Canto 63.

Metre: – – – – ᴜ – – – ᴜ ᴜ ᴜ ᴜ ᴜ – – – ᴜ – – – ᴜ – ๏
21 feet, sragdharā.

1. eñjiṇ çrī nātha warṇnan/ mijil apupul aweḥ sewa riṇ bhṛtya māntrī,
āryyadinyaṇ maṛkh/ mwaṇ para patih atathā riṇ witānan paliṅgiḥ,
ṅkā saṇ mā- (*119a*) ntryāpatiḥ wīra gajamada maṛk
[sapraṇamyādarojar,
an wantĕn/ rājakāryyālihulihn ikanaṇ ḍāryya haywa pramāda.

2. ājñā çrī nātha saṇ çrī tribhūwana wijayottuṅgadewī ....
çraddā çrī rājapātnī wkasana gawayĕn/ çrī narendreṇ kaḍatwan,
siddāniṇ kāryya riṇ çāka diwaça maçiraḥ warṇna riṇ bhadramāsa,
sakweḥ çrī nātha rakwāwwata taḍaḥ iriṅĕn de para wṛḍḍamantrī.

3. nāhan liṇ saṇ sumantri tka subhaya maweḥ tuṣta ri çrī narendrā,
sontĕn prāptomaṛk taṇ para ḍapur aputiḥ sujyanāḍinya wijñā,
mwaṇ mantry āsiṇ wineḥ thānya suruhana makādyāryya rāmāḍirāja,
tan len göṇ niṇ byayānu sinaḍasaḍa ginoṣti haṛp/ çrī narendrā.

4. byātitan meḥ tkaṇ bhadrapada ri tiḷmniṇ çrāwaṇo teki warṇnan,
sakweḥnyaṇ citrakārā nikanikĕl amaṅun/ sthāna siṅheṇ waṅuntur,
dūdwaṇ mālad/ wawan bhojana bukubukuran/ mwaṇ tapĕl saprakāra,
milwaṇ paṇḍe ḍaḍap/ kāñcana rājata paḍewĕr mmatāmbĕh
[swakāryya.

Canto 64.

Metre: – – – ᴜ ᴜ – – ᴜ – ᴜ ᴜ ᴜ – – – – ᴜ – – ᴜ ๏
19 feet, çārdūlawikrīḍita.

1. ndaḥ prāptaṇ çubhakhala sāmpun atitaḥ tekaṇ sabhānindita,
ṅkāne maḍya witāna çobhita rinĕṅga lwir prisaḍyāruhur,
tuṅgal taṇ mabatur çi- (*119b*) lāsaka rinaktārjja wuwuṇ hinyasan,
saçryāpan/ paḍa muṅgwi sanmukha nikaṇ siṅhāsanātyādbhutā.

2. kulwan maṇḍapa sapralamba winaṅun/ sthānā narendrāpupul,
   lor tekaṇ taratag/ piṇik miḍĕr amūrwwātumpatumpa wugat,
   strīniṇ māntri bhūjaṅga wipraṅ inahā talphanya sāmpun pĕpĕk,
   ṅkāne dakṣiṇa bhṛtyasaṅghya taratagnya saṅkya kīrṇnāsusun.

3. ndan tiṅkaḥ ni gawe narendra wkasiṇ sarwwajñapūjāḍikā,
   sakweḥ saṇ wiku boḍḍa tantragata sākṣiṇ maṇḍalā lekanā,
   mūkyā sthāpaka saṇ purohita maṣadpāde suḍarmme naḍī,
   labḍāwega çuçilā satwika tĕtĕs/ riṇ çāstratantratrayā.

4. saṅke wṛḍḍanirān/ sahaçramāsa riṇ swotpatti maṅgöṇ tutur,
   wwantĕn hīnanireṇ swakāya khimutaṇ sātçiṣya makweḥ mark,
   ṅkā mpuṅkwiṇ paruha prasidḍa pataṅan lāmpahnireṇ maṇḍalā,
   mudrā mantra japānut uḍara minuṣṭyāṅde tĕpĕtniṇ hiḍĕp.

5. taṅgal piṇ rwawlas maṅiñjĕm irika swaḥ sutrapāteniwö,
   mwaṇ homārccana len pariçramā samāpte prāptaniṇ swaḥ muwaḥ,
   saṇ hyaṇ puspa yinoga ri wñi linakwan/ supratiṣṭakriyā,
   pöh niṇ ḍyana samāḍi sidḍi kinnākĕn de (120a) mahāsthāpakā.

Canto 65.

Metre: – – – ◡ ◡ – ◡ – ◡ ◡ ◡ – ◡◡ ◡ ◡ ◡ ◡ – ◡ – ◡ ∽
23 feet, *jagaddhita.*

1. eñjiṇ pūrṇnamakāla kālani wijilnira pinark i maḍyaniṇ sabhā,
   ghūrṇnaṇ kāhala çāṅka len paḍaha gāñjaran i harp açaṅkya
                                        [maṇdulur,
   riṇ siṅhāsana çobhitāruhur/ mānuṣa kahananirān/ winūrṣitā,
   sakweḥ saṇ para sogatānwam atuhā tlas apuphul/ hamūjā sakramā.

2. ṅkā ta çrī nṛpatin/ parṇ mark amuspa saha tathanaya dāra sādā,
   milwaṇ mantry apatiḥ gajamada makādinika paḍa masomahān mark,
   mwaṇ mantryākuwu riṇ pamiṅgir atawā para ratu sahaneṇ
                                        [digantarā,
   sāmpunyān/ paḍa bhakty amūrṣita paliṅgihan ikā tinitaḥ
                                        [yathākramā.

4

3. çrī nātheŋ paguhan sirekhi rumuhun/ humaturakĕn anindya bhojanā,
saŋ çrī handiwa handiwa lwir i tapĕl niran amawa dukūla len/ sĕṛh,
çrī nātheŋ matawun tapĕlnira sitawṛṣabha hanam amiṇḍa nandinī,
yekāmĕtwakĕn ārtha bhojana mijil/ saka ri tutuk apūrwwa tan/
[pgat..

4. saŋ çrī nātha ri wĕṅkĕr apnĕd awawān/ yaça pathani taḍahnirāḍikā,
sarwwendaḥ racananya mūlya madulūr danawitaraṇa wartta riŋ
[sabhā,
çrī nātheṅ tumapĕl tapĕlnira kaṅ endah araras açarira kāmi-
[(120b) ni,
kāpwā teki matuṅgalan/ dina sirān pawijil i kawicitraniŋ manaḥ.

5. mukyā çrī narapatyapūrwwa giri manḍara wawanira bhojanādbhutā,
kālanyān/ pinutĕr tapĕl/ wiwuḍa daityagaṇa miḍĕr aṛs twasiŋ
[mihāt,
lmborātyaya göŋnya kāhinawa polaman aṅbĕk aliwran aŋdulur,
kādyāgraḥ mawĕṛ tkapni bañuniŋ tasik amĕwĕhi rāmyaniŋ sabhā.

6. ndan naṅkĕn dina salwiriŋ tapĕl asing lwih adika niwedya donikā,
strīniŋ mantry upapatti wipra dinumān/ sakari nikha duwĕg
[matuṅgalan,
mwaŋ saŋ kṣatriya wanḍawa nṛpati mukya sira rinawĕhān
[sasāmbhawā,
len saṅkeŋ wara bhojanedĕridĕr edran i sabala narendrā riŋ sabhā.

Canto 66.

Metre: - - - ◡ ◡ - ◡ - ◡ ◡ ◡ - ◡ ◡ ◡ ◡ - - ◡ - ◡ ◡ ◡ ෙ
25 feet, a kind of atikṛti.

1. eñjiŋ rakwa khapiŋ nĕm iŋ dina bhaṭāra narapati sabhojanākrama
[maṛk,
mwaŋ saŋ kṣatriya saŋ paḍāḍika pnuḥ yaça bukubukuran rinĕmbat
[asusun,
darmmādyakṣa kaliḥ sirekhin awawan/ banawa paḍa winarṇna
[bhawakha khiduŋ,
göŋnyā lwir tuhu phalwa goŋ bubar agĕnturan aṅiriṅ aweḥ
[ṛsĕpniṅ umulat.

2. rākryan/ saŋ mapatiḥ gajamada rikaŋ dina muwah ahatur
[niwedyan umaṛk,
(121a) stryāṅgöŋ çokha tapĕlnirārjja ri hĕbiŋ bhūjagakusuma
[rājaçāçrañawilt,
mantryāryyāsuruhan/ pradeça milu len/ para ḍapur ahatur
[niwedyan añiriŋ,
akweḥ lwirni wawanya bhojana hanan/ plawa giri yaça mātsya
[tanpa pgatan.

3. atyadbhūta haḷpni kāryya naranātha wkas i wkasiŋ mahottama
[dahat,
āpan riŋ dina sapta tan pgat tikaŋ ḍana waçana sabhojanāparimitā,
lumre saŋ catur açrama pramukha saŋ dwija milu para mantry
[asaṅkya kasukhan,
kahyunhyun/ juru samyāmalwaṅ atpa tkap i larih ika lwir āmbut
[umilī.

4. sar sök tekhaṅ aniṅhaniṅhali sakeŋ daçadikh atĕtĕl atri tanpa
[ligaran.
tiṅkaḥ niŋ pasabhān/ lawan saṅ ahatur ttaḍah atiki tinonyan açraṅ
[aṛbut,
çrī rājyā rikanaŋ witāna maṅigĕl bini bini juga taŋ maniṅhali maṛk,
kāpwā liṅgih atiṇḍih aglar aṅbĕk hana lali riṅ ulaḥ kawöñan umulat.

5. sāsiŋ kāryya maweha tuṣṭa rikanaŋ para jana winañun nareçwara
[huwus,
naŋ wīdwāmacañaḥ rakĕt rakĕt añanti sahāna para gītada pratidinā,
ānyāt/ *(121b)* bhāṭa mapatra yudḍa sahajaŋ maglaglapan aṅghyat
[aŋdani pacĕh,
mūkyaŋ ḍāna ri salwiriŋ manasi tan pgat amuhara harṣaniŋ
[sabhūwanā.

Canto 67.

Metre: - - - ‿ ‿ - ‿ - ‿ ‿ - - - ‿ - - - ‿ - ◦
20 feet, a kind of kṛti.

1. yāwat/ maṅka lkas narendrā magawe çradḍāñiwö saŋ paratra,
tāwat tan/ pakawaṇḍya kaṅdaniŋ sukhe çrī rājapatnīn kināryya,
āstwāṅdadyakna ryyanugrahanire swasthānyadĕg/ çrī narendrā,
saŋ çrī rājasanāgarāstu jayaçatrwāhīñanaŋ candra sūryya.

2. eñjiŋ kāla ḍataŋ mamūja para boddāṅūrakĕn saŋ pinūjā,
   prajñāparimitā tmahniran umantuk/ rī mahābuddaloka,
   saŋhyaŋ puspa çarīra çīghra linarūt/ sāmpun muliḥ sopakāra,
   sakweḥ cāru gañjaran tuwi dinūm/ lumrerikaŋ bhṛtyasaṅghya.

3. līlā çūḍḍa manaḥ narendrā ri huwusni kāryya noraŋ wikhalpa,
   aṅhiŋ ḍarmmanireki pinrih i kamal paṇḍak/ ri dadyanya pūrṇna,
   tkwān/ sāmpun abhūmiçūḍḍa rikanaŋ çakāgni saptārkka ṅūntĕn,
   saŋ çrī jñānawiḍin lumakwani t-hĕr/ mabrāhmayajñan pamūjā.

———

Canto 68.

Metre: – – – ◡ ◡ – – ◡ – ◡ ◡ ◡ – – – – ◡ – – ◡ ⌣
19 feet, *çārdūlawikrīḍita.*

1. nāhan tatwanikaŋ kamal/ wiḍita deniŋ sāmpradāya sthīti,
   mwaŋ çrī pañjalunātha riŋ daha tĕ- (*122a*) wĕkniŋ yāwabhūmy/
   [āpaliḥ,
   çrī airlaṅghya siraṅdani ryyasihirān/ panak/ ri saŋ rwa prabhū.*

2. wwantĕn bodḍa mahāyanabrata pgat/ riŋ tantra yogiçwara,
   saŋ muṅgwiŋ tṅah i çmaçāna ri lmaḥ citrenusir niŋ jagat,
   saŋ prāpteŋ bali toyamārgga manapak/ wwainiŋ tasik nirbhaya,
   kyātiŋ hyaŋ mpu bharaḍa woḍa ri hatītādi trikālāpagĕḥ.

3. rāhyaŋ tekhi pinintakāsihan amarwaŋ bhūmi tan laṅghyana,
   iṅānyeki tlas/ cinīhnanira toyeŋ kuṇḍi saṅkeŋ laṅit,
   kūlwān/ pūrwwa dudug riṅ ārṇnawa maparwaŋ lor kidul tan
   [madoḥ,
   kādyādoḥ mahlĕt/ samudra tĕwĕkiŋ bhūmi jawa rwa prabhū.

4. ṅkai riŋ tik/tiki wṛkṣa rakwa sutapārāryyan/ saṅkeŋ āmbara,
   naŋ deçeŋ paluṅān tikaŋ pasalahan/ kuṇḍi praçāsteŋ jagat,
   kāṇḍĕg/ deni ruhur nikaŋ kamāl i puñcaknyāṅawit/ cīwara,
   nā hetunya sināpa dadyalita tĕkwan/ muṅgwiri pāntara.

———

*) this stanza has only 3 verses.

5. tūgwāṅgöḥ nika tāmbayiṇ jana paḍāṛs mintareṇ swāsana,
   etūnyān/ winaṅun suḍarmma waluyaṇ bhūmi jawātuṅgalā,
   sthītyārāja sabhūmī kawruhananiṅ rāt (122b) dlāha tan liṅgara,
   cīhnā çrī nṛpatin jayeṇ sakhalabhūmin/ cakrawartti prabhū.

(Between canto 68 and canto 69 the double pada is missing.)

Canto 69.

Metre: – – – ◡ ◡ – ◡ – ◡ ◡ ◡ – – – – ◡ – – ◡ – ๑
20 feet, a kind of kṛti.

1. prajñāpārimitāpurī ywa panlahniṅ rāt/ ri saṇhyaṇ suḍarmma,
   prajñāpāramitākriyenulahakĕn/ çrī jñānawiḍyapratiṣṭā,
   sotan/ paṇḍita wṛdḍa tantragata lābḍaweça sarwwāgamajñā,
   sākṣat/ hyaṇ mpu bharaḍa māwak i sirāṅde tṛpti ki twas narendrā.

2. mwaṇ taiki ri bhayālaṅö ṅgwanira saṇ çrī rājapatnin ḍinarmmā,
   rahyaṇ jñānawiḍīnutus/ muwah amūjā bhūmi çudḍā pratiṣṭā,
   etūnyān maṅaran/ wiçeṣapura khārambhānya pinriḥ ginöṇ twas,
   mantryāgöṇ winkas/ wruherikha dmuṇ bhoja nwam ūtsāha wijñā.

3. lumrā sthānanirān pinūjā winaṅun/ caityāḍi riṇ sarwwadeçā,
   yāwat/ waiçapurī pakuwwana kabhaktyan/ çrī mahārājapatnī,
   aṅkĕn bhādra sirān pinūjaniṇ amatya brāhmā sakweḥnya bhakti,
   mūktī swargganirān/ mapotraka wiçeṣaṇ yāwabhūmyekhanātha.

54

CHAPTER 10 - SIMPING.

Canto 70.

Metre: ⌣ ⌣ ⌣ ⌣ ⌣ — — — — — — ⌣ — ⌣ ⌣ — ⌣ ●
17 feet, hariṇī.

1. irikaṅ anilāṣṭānaḥ çāka nṛpeçwara warṇnanĕn,
   mahasahas i simpiṅ saṅhyaṅ ḍarmma rakwa sirālihĕn,
   saha wiḍiwiḍānāsiṅ lwir/ niṅ (*123a*) saji krama tan kuraṅ,
   prakhaçita saṅ adyakṣāmūjāryya rājaparākrama.

2. rasika nipuṇeṅ widyā tatwopadeça çiwāgami,
   sira ta maṅaḍiṣṭāne saṅ çrī nṛpa kṛtarājasa,
   duwĕg inulahakĕn taṅ prāsāda gopurā mekāla,
   prakaçita saṅ āryyānāma kruṅ prayatna wineḥ wruha.

3. nṛpatin umuliḥ saṅke simpiṅ wawaṅ ḍatĕñ iṅ purā,
   prihati tkap iṅ griṅ saṅ mantryāḍīmantra gajamada,
   rasika sahakārī wṛḍḍyāniṅ yawāwani riṅ daṅū,
   ri bali ri saḍeṅ wyaktinyantuknikānayakĕn/ musuḥ.

CHAPTER 11 - GAJAH MADA.

Canto 71.

Metre: ◡ ◡ ◡ ◡ – ◡ – ◡ ◡ ◡ – – ◡ – ◡ ◡ – ◡ – ◡ ◡ ◡ ◠
23 feet, açwalalita.

1. try añin ina çāka pūrwwa rasikan/ pamaṅkwakn i sabwatiŋ
   [sabhūwana,
   pjah irika çākābḍa rasa tanwināça naranātha mār salahaça,
   tuhun i kadiwyacittanira tan/ satṛṣṇam asih i samāsta bhūwana,
   hatutur i tatwaniŋ dadin anitya puṇya juga taŋ ginöŋ pratidina.

2. kunaŋ i pahĕm narendrā haji rāmā saŋ prabhū kaliḥ sireki pinupul,
   hibu haji saŋ rwa tansah awawānuja nṛpati karwa saŋ priya tumūt,
   gumunita saŋ wruheŋ gumuṇadoṣaniŋ bala gumantyane saṅ apatiḥ,
   linawĕlawön datan hana katṛptiniŋ twas amaṅun/ wiyoga sumusuk.

3. nṛ- (*123b*) pati sumimpĕn iŋ naya tatan kagantyana kta sumantri
   [mapatiḥ,
   ri taya nikaŋ gumantya yadi kewĕhanya tikanaŋ jagat pahalalun,
   ṅhiṅ ikaṅ amātya sādwajara sarwwa kāryya satate narendrā pilihĕn,
   pituhanĕn iŋ mucap kirakira wruheŋ parawiwoda tanpa nūsara.

Canto 72.

Metre: – ‿ – ‿ ‿ ‿ – ‿ ‿ – ‿
11 feet, swagatā.

1. maṅka hīnaniṅ pahömnira guptā,
   pöhnyalap/ knanirān pawiweka,
   wṛḍḍamāntri piniliḥ ta saṅ āryya,
   ātmarāja makanāma pu taṇḍi.

2. tansah iṇḍika narendrā saṅ āryya,
   wīra maṇḍalika nāma pu nāla,
   sāḍwasāḍu hitanigraha wijñā,
   mañcanāgara manama tumĕṅguṅ.

3. tusniṅ āḍiguṇa wira susatya,
   nityasāḍipatiniṅ bala maṅdon,
   naṅ digantara manāma riṅ ḍompo,
   bhraṣṭa denira sĕk anaṅlwaṅ i çatru.

4. rwā ta wastuniṅ wangāḍisumantrī,
   aṣṭapadḍa haji donika tan len,
   mawwate sarusitiṅ wyawahāra,
   ndan makeriṅa sumantry upapatī.

5. saṅ pati dami tikaṅ yuwamantrī,
   saṅ hinatyan i daḷm/ pura tansaḥ,
   mwaṅ patiḥ tikaṅ anāma pu singhā,
   sākṣya riṅ sabha wkas naranātha.

6. an maṅkana titaḥ naranātha,
   tṛpti laṅgĕṅ hapagöḥ tikanaṅ rā- *(124a)* t,
   satya bhakti nika maṅkin atambĕḥ,
   keçwaran haji dumeḥ nika maṅkā.

———

CHAPTER 12 - DOMAINS.

Canto 73.

Metre: – ◡ ◡ – ◡ – ◡ ◡ ◡ – ◡ – ◡ ◡ ◡ – – ◡ – ◡ ◡ ◡ ⏑
22 feet, madraka.

1. ndan/ nṛpa tiktawilwapurarāja maṅkin atiyatnā nīti riṅ ulaḥ,
   riŋ wyawahāra tan hana khasiṅhin iṅ hati sapöhniṅ agama tinūt,
   tan dadi pākṣapāta yat aweḥ wibhūti saniruktya riŋ jana kabeḥ,
   kīrtti ginöŋnirān wruh iṅ anāgatādi tuhu dewamūrtti sakāla.

2. ṅkā tikanaŋ suḍarmma haji suk ni saŋ tuhatuhā nareçwara daṅū,
   sālwirika turuŋ pinahuwusnirenapi rinakṣa pinrih iniwö,
   siŋ katayan/ praçāsti winkas/ praçāstyana ri saŋ widagḍa riṅ aji,
   sthitya phalanya tanpa tmaha wiwāda tumuse satusnira hlĕm.

3. kweḥnikanaŋ suḍarmma haji kaprakāçita makhadi riŋ kagnĕṅan,
   lwir nikanaŋ maṅādi tumapĕl/ kiḍal/ jajagu wĕḍwawĕḍwan i tuḍan,
   mwaŋ pikatan bukul jawajawāntaṅ antaraçaçī kālaŋ brat i jaga,
   len balitar/ çilāhrit i waleri babĕg i kukap ri lumbaṅ i pagör.

Canto 74.

Metre: – – – ◡ ◡ ◡ ◡ – – ◡ – ◡ – ⏑
13 feet, praharṣiṇī.

1. mukyāntaḥpura sagalāthawā ri simpiŋ,
   mwaŋ çrī raṅgapura muwaḥ riŋ buḍḍi kuñcir,
   prajñāpāramita purī hañar panambĕḥ,
   mwaŋ tekaŋ ri bhayalanö duwĕg kināryya.

2. (124b) nā taŋ ḍarmma haji wilaŋ saptāwiṅça,
   riŋ sapta dwija rawi çāka bhadramāsa,
   kapwāmātya nipuṇa taŋ wineḥ matuṅgwa,
   lāwan/ sthāpaka wiku rājya çāstrawijña.

Canto 75.

Metre: - - - ⌣ ⌣ - ⌣ - ⌣ ⌣ ⌣ - - - - - ⌣ - - ⌣ - ͜
20 feet, a kind of kṛti.

1. ndan saŋ mantri wineḥ wruhā rika kabeḥ saṅ āryya wīrāḍikāra,
   ḍarmmādyakṣa rumakṣa salwir ikanaŋ ḍarmme daḷm tan pramāda,
   ḍirotsāha nitya kuminkin i swasthā parārttha saŋ çrī narendrā,
   tan/ mūkti phalaniŋ swakāryya ri gĕñany utpatti saŋ hyaŋ
                                          [suḍarmma.
2. len taŋ ḍarmma lpas paḍekana rinakṣādĕgnya de çrī narendrā,
   çaiwaḍyakṣa sira wineḥ wruha rumakṣa parhyaṅan/ mwaŋ kalagyan,
   boḍḍādyakṣa sireki rakṣaka ri sakweḥniŋ kuṭi mwaŋ wihāra,
   mantrī her haji taŋ karṣyan iniwönyān/ rakṣeka saŋ tapaswi.

Canto 76.

Metre: - - - ⌣ ⌣ - ⌣ - ⌣ ⌣ ⌣ - ⌣ ⌣ ⌣ ⌣ ⌣ - - ⌣ - ⌣ ⌣ ⌣ ͜
25 feet, a kind of atikṛti.

1. lwir ni ḍarmma lpas/ pratiṣṭa çiwa mukya kuṭi balay i kañci len
                                          [kapuluṅan,
   roma mwaŋ wwatan īçwaragṛha phalabḍi tajuŋ i kuṭi lamba len/
                                          [ri taruṇa,
   parhyaṅan kuṭi jāti caṇḍi lima nīlakusuma harinanḍanottama suka,
   mwaŋ prāsāda hajī saḍaŋ muwah i paṅgumulan i kuṭi saṅgrahe
                                          [jayaçikā.

2. tan karyya sphaṭikeyaṅ i jaya manalwi haribhawana caṇḍi (125a)
                                          [wuṅkal i pigit,
   nyū dante katude sraṅan/ kapuyuran jayamuka kulanandane
                                          [kanigara,
   ṛmbut lan wuluhĕn muwaḥ ri khinawöŋ mwaṅ i sukhawijayāthawā
                                          [ri kajaha,
   campĕn/ mwaŋ ratimānmathāçrama kula kaliṅ i batu putiḥ tekha
                                          [pamĕwĕḥ.

3. lwirniŋ ḍarmma kasogatan kawinayanu ḷpas i wipularāma len kuṭi
[haji,
mwaŋ yānatraya rājaḍanya kuwunātha surayaça jarak/ laguṇḍi
[wadari,
wewe mwaŋ packan/ pasarwwan i lmaḥ surat i pamaṇikan/
[sraṅan/ paṅiktan,
paṅhapwan/ damalaŋ tpas/ jita waṇnaçrama jnar i samudrawela
[pamuluŋ.

4. baryyaŋ ṅamr̥tawardḍanī wtiwtiḥ kawinayan i patĕmwan iŋ
[kanuruhan,
wĕṅtal/ wĕṅkĕr i hantĕn iŋ bañu jikĕn/ batabata pagagan/ sibok/
[paduruṅan,
mwaŋ piṇḍātuha len/ tlaŋ surabha mukyanika ri sukalīla tapwa
[pamĕwĕḥ,
tan warṇnan tikanaŋ maṅanwaya ri pogara ri kulur i taṅkil ādi
[nika sön.

Canto 77.

Mctre: – – ᴗ – ᴗ ᴗ ᴗ – ᴗ – ᴗ ᴗ ᴗ ᴗ – ᴗ – ᴗ ᴗ ᴗ ᴗ ᴗ
20 feet, a kind of kr̥ti.

1. nāhan muwaḥ kasugatan/ kabajraḍaran akrameka wuwusĕn,
i çākabajra ri nadī tada mwaṅ i mukuḥ ri sāmbaṅ i tajuŋ,
lāwan taṅ amr̥tasabha ri baŋbaṅirī boḍḍi (*125b*) mula waharu,
tāmpak/ ḍuri paruha taṇḍare kumudaratna nandināgara.

2. len taŋ wuṅañjayā palaṇḍit aṅkil asah iŋ samicyapitahĕn,
nairañjane wijayawaktra magnĕṅ i poyahan/ bala masin,
ri krat lĕmaḥ tulis i ratnapaṅkaja panumbaṅan kahuripan,
mwaŋ ketaki talaga jambale juṅul i wiṣṇuwāla pamĕwĕḥ.

3. len tekaŋ buḍur wwirun i wuṅkulur mwaṅ i manaṅguṅ i watu kura,
bajrāsana mwaṅ i pajambayan/ ri samalantĕn iŋ simapurā,
tambak laleyan i pilaṅgu poh aji ri waṅkali mwaṅ i bĕru,
ḷmbaḥ dalīnan i paṅadwan ādi nika riŋ pacaccan apagöḥ.

Canto 78.

Metre: - - - ◡ ◡ - ◡ - ◡ ◡ - - - - ◡ - - ◡ ●
19 feet, çārdūlawikrīḍita.

1. lwir niŋ ḍarmma lpas karṣyan i sumpud/ rupit/ mwaŋ pilan,
   len tekaŋ pucañan/ jagadḍita pawitra mwaŋ butun tan kasaḥ,
   kapwā teka hana pratiṣṭa çabha len liṅga praṇālāpupul,
   mpuṅku sthāpaka saŋ mahāguru paněṅguḥ ni sarāt/ kotama.

2. yekiŋ ḍarmma lpas/ rinakṣa mapagöḥ riŋ swakramanyeŋ dañū,
   milwaŋ sīma ta pratiṣṭa pinakādinyan/ swatantra sthiti,
   bañwan tuṅkal i siḍḍayatra jaya len siḍḍāhajöŋ lwaḥ (126a) kali,
   twas/ wāçiṣṭa palaḥ padar siriñan ādinyaŋ kaçewāṅkurān.

3. wañjaŋ bajrapure wanora makduk hantěn/ guhā mwaŋ jiwa,
   jumput/ çobha pamuntaran/ baru kaboḍḍāñçan/ prakāçottama,
   kajar ddāna haña turas/ jalagiri cěṇṭiŋ wkas/ waṇḍira,
   waṇḍayan gatawaŋ kulampayan i tālādinya kaṣyaṅkura.

4. ḍarmmārṣī sawuñan/ blaḥ juru siḍḍaŋ srāñan waduryyāglan,
   gaṇḍātṛp haraçāla nampu kakadaŋ hajyan gahan riŋ jagat,
   sīmā nadyabhaye tiyaŋ pakuwukan/ sīmā kiyal/ mwaŋ çucī,
   tan karyyaŋ kawirī barat/ kacapañan/ ywāṅěhnya simāpagöḥ.

5. len saṅkerika wañça wiṣṇu kālatiŋ batwan kamañsyan batu,
   taṅulyān/ ḍakulut galuḥ makalaran/ mukya swatantrāpagöḥ,
   len taŋ deça mḍaŋ hulun/ hyaṅ i paruŋ luṅge pasajyan kělūt,
   anděl mād paraḍaḥ gnöŋ pañawan ādinyan luput riŋ dañū.

6. tan warṇnan tikanaŋ kalagyan anlat/ riŋ sarwwa deçeŋ jawā,
   lāwan taŋ kuṭi sapratiṣṭa milu taŋ tanpa prātiṣṭāpagöḥ,
   ndan/ bhedanya kasaṅhikān/ sthiti kabhūktyanyān sake nāgara,
   (126b) mwaŋ kasthāpakan uṅwaniŋ lumagi lagy amriḥ kriya
   [mwaŋ brata.

7. len taŋ maṇḍala mūla sāgara kukub/ pūrwwasthitinyeniwö,
   tan karyyaŋ sukayajña kasturi caturbhaṣmeka liŋ saŋ ṛṣī,
   katyāgan/ caturaçrame pacira bulwan/ mwaŋ luwan/ ṇwe kupaŋ,
   akweh lrānya mañaçrayeŋ thani lawan/ jaṅgan/ prasidḍeŋ jagat.

CHAPTER 13 - ORGANIZATION OF THE CLERGY.

Canto 79.

Metre: – – – – ◡ – – – ◡ ◡ ◡ ◡ ◡ – – ◡ – – ◡ – ◔
21 feet, sragdharā.

1. sāmpun taŋ sarwwadeçeŋ jawa tinapak adĕgnyeki ńunin linakwan.
   darmma mwaŋ sīma len/ wańça hilahila hulun hyaŋ kuṭi mwaŋ
   [kalagyan,
   sakweḥniŋ sapramāṇa pinagĕhaknasiŋ nispramaṇa gin-gwan,
   māntuk/ riŋ deça bhṛtyan sinalahakn i saŋ ńāryya rāmādirāja.

2. çrī nātheŋ wĕńkĕr otus manapakā rikanaŋ deça sakweḥnya warṇnan,
   çrī nātheŋ sińhasāryy otus anapaka ri göŋniŋ ḍapur saprakāra,
   kapwāgögwan/ patik/ guṇḍala siran umiwö kāryya tan lambalamba,
   hetunyaŋ yāwabhūmy ātutur iń ulah anūt/ çaçāna çri narendrā.

3. ńkā taŋ nūṣantare bāly amatĕhati sācāraniŋ yāwabhūmī,
   darmmā mwaŋ çrama lawwan/ kuwu tinapak adĕg/ nyeki sampun
   [tininkaḥ,
   saŋ boḍḍādyakṣa muńgwi baḍahu- (127a) lu baḍahalwāŋ gajaḥ
   [tan pramāda,
   wruh rī kwehniŋ suḍarmme kasugatan inutus/ çrī narendrān/
   [rumakṣā.

Canto 80.

Metre: – ◡ ◡ – ◡ – ◡ ◡ ◡ – ◡ – ◡ ◡ ◡ – ◡ – ◡ ◡ ◡ ◔
22 feet, madraka.

1. lwir nikanaŋ kasogatan i bāli kāḍikaraṇan/ muwaḥ kuṭi hañar,
   lāwan i pūrwwanāgara muwaḥ wihāra bahuń ādirajya kuturan,
   nöm tikanaŋ kabajraḍaran ūttama ńhiń i wihāra taŋ kawinayan,
   kīrṇna makadiń āryya dadi rājasanmata kuṭinya tan wicaritan.

2. milwa tikaŋ suḍarmma ri bukhit/ sulaŋ ḷmah i lampuṅ anyawasuḍā,
    kyātyaṅaran tathāgatapura gṛhaswāḍara supraçāstin amatöḥ,
    bhyoma rasākka çāka diwaçanya suk/ nṛpati jiwāneçwara daṅū,
    wṛdḍa sumantry upāsakaṅ abhūmiçūdḍa t-hĕr apratiṣṭan inutus.

3. salwir ikaŋ swatantra tuhu sapramaṇa pagöḥ tkap narapatī,
    kirtti saṅ ādi sajjana çākāwakhanya ya rinakṣa mogha tinṅöt,
    maṅka juga swabhawa saṅ inuttama prabhū wiçeṣa digjaya wibhūḥ,
    nyāma muwaḥ rinakṣa sahanāni kirttinira deni saŋ prabhū hlĕm.

4. mwaŋ makadon/ katona taya ni durātmaka rikaŋ sabhūmi kacaya,
    hetu nikaŋ pradeça tinapak/ tinutlas awaḷr samudra jinajaḥ,
    (127b) sthityaniraŋ tapaswi sahaneŋ pasir wukir alas/ pradeça
                                           [kasnĕt,
    tṛptyamiwö tapa brata samādyanambyakn i haywaniŋ sabhūwana.

Canto 81.

Metre: – – – ◡ ◡ – ◡ – ◡ ◡ ◡ – ◡ – – – ◡ ◔
17 feet, a kind of atyaṣṭi.

1. göŋnyārambha nareçware pagĕha saŋ tripakṣe jawa,
    pūrwwācāranireŋ praçāstyalama taŋ rinakṣan iwö,
    kotsāhan haji yatna donira wineḥ patik guṇḍala,
    tan wismṛtyanireŋ carādigama çikṣa len/ çaçāna.

2. nāhan kāraṇa saŋ caturdwija paḍāṅusir kottaman,
    wipra mwaŋ ṛṣi çaiwā bodḍā tgĕpiŋ swawidyātutur,
    sakweḥ saŋ catur açrama pramukha saŋ catu bhaṣma sök,
    kapwā teka tumuṅkul iŋ brata widagḍa riŋ swakriyā.

3. ṅkā sakweḥnira saŋ caturjjana paḍāsthitiŋ çaçāna,
    mantrī mukya saṅ āryya karwa nipuṇeŋ kabhūphālakan,
    kryan/ kryan/ kṣatriya waṅça len wali suçilā yatneŋ naya,
    milwaŋ weçya sabhūmi çūdra jnĕk swakāryyāpagöḥ.

4. yekaŋ janmi catur sujanman umijil/ sakeŋ hyaŋ wiḍī,
    liŋniŋ çāstra wnaŋ sagatyanika de narendreŋ pura,
    kapwekāpagĕh iŋ swaçilā kimutaŋ kujanma traya,
    naŋ caṇḍāla mĕleca tucca paḍa yatna riŋ swakrama.

Canto 82.

Metre: – – .. – ◡ – – ◡ ◡ ◡ ◡ ◡ – .. – ◡ ◡ ◡ ◠
20 feet, suwadanā.

1. an ma- (*128a*) ṅkā lwir nikaŋ bhūmi jawa ri paṅadĕg/ çrī nātha
                                                        [siniwī,
   nora sandeha ri twasniran umulahakĕn/ kīrttyānukani rāt,
   tkwan/ çrī nātha kārwāmwaṅ i hajin agawe saddarmma kuçala,
   mwaŋ penan/ çrī narendrā pranuha tumut i buddi çrī narapati.

2. çrī nāthe siṅhasāryyānaruka ri sagaḍā ḍarmma parimita,
   çrī nātheŋ wĕṅkĕr iŋ çūrabhana pasuruhan/ lāwan taṅ i pajaŋ,
   buddādiṣṭāna tekaŋ rawa ri kapuluṅan/ mwaŋ locanapurā,
   çrī nāthe watsarīkaŋ tigawaṅi magawe tuṣṭeŋ para jana.

3. sakwehniŋ mantri sampun/ kṛtawara sinuṅan sīmāsirasirān,
   caitya prasāda tapwaŋ ginaway ika lawan liṅāḍi satata,
   bhaktiŋ hyaŋ bhakti ri pitṛgaṇa samasamātwaŋ riŋ muniwara,
   dāna mwaŋ kīrtti puṇyenulahakn ika solah saŋ prabhū tinūt.

64

CHAPTER 14 - THE COURT FESTIVAL.

Canto 83.

Metre: - - - - ◡ - - - ◡ ◡ ◡ ◡ ◡ - - - - - - ◡ - ◒
21 feet, sragdharā.

1. an maṅkā kottaman/ çrī narapati siniwiŋ tiktawilwaikanātha,
   sākṣāt/ candreŋ sarat/ kastawaniran agawe tuṣṭaniŋ sarwwaloka,
   lwir padmaŋ durjjana lwir kumuda sahana saŋ sājanāsiḥ tke twas,
   bhṛtya mwaŋ koça leṇ/ wāhana ga- (*128b*) ja turagādinya himpěr
   [samudra.

2. maṅkin/ rabdekana yāwaḍaraṇi kapawitranya riŋ rāt/ prakāça,
   ṅhiŋ jambudwīpa lāwan/ yawa ktaṅ inucap/ kottamanyan/ sudeça,
   dcniŋ kweḥ saŋ widagdeṅ aji makamukha saŋ ḍyakṣa saptopapatti,
   mwaŋ pañjyaŋ jīwa lekan taṅar asiṅ umuṅūp kāryya kapwātidakṣa.

3. mukyaŋ çrī brahmarāja dwijawara mamahākawy anindyāŋ gamajña,
   hěntyaŋ tarkkādi kawruḥniraŋ nipuṇa mahākawya naiyeyikādī,
   mwaŋ ḍaṅhyaŋ bhāmanātibrata kuçala tameŋ weda ṣad karmma
   [çūḍḍa,
   astam/ çrī wiṣṇu çakte samajapa makhadon/ wṛḍḍyaniŋ rāt/
   [subhikṣa.

4. hetunyānantara sarwwajana tka sakeṅ anyadeça prakīrṇna,
   naŋ jambudwipa khamboja cina yawana len/ cěmpa kharṇnātakadī,
   goḍa mwaŋ syaṅka taŋ saṅkanika makahawan/ potra milwiŋ
   [waṇikh sök,
   bhikṣu mwaŋ wipra mukyān hana tka sinuṅan/ bhoga tuṣṭan
   [pañanti.

5. ndān aṅkěn phalguṇa çrī nṛpati pinaripūjeniwö riŋ swarājya,
   prāptaŋ mantri sabhūmī jawa juru kuwu len ḍyakṣa sarwwopapatti,
   milwaŋ bālyādi nūṣāntara sahana saha prabhṛtin tan pgat sökh,
   byā- (*129a*) pārī mwaŋ waṇiṅ/ ri pkěn aṅěběk atip/ sarwwa
   [baṇḍanya kīrṇna.

6. tiṅkahniṅ pūjan idran/ bhrisaḍi saha mṛdaṅgenarak niṅ waṅ akweḥ,
    piṅ pitwāṅkĕn dinaimbuḥ sasikhi saha niwaidyan dunuṅ riṅ
                                                        [wañuntur,
    homa mwaṅ brahmayajñenulahaknira saṅ çewa boḍḍan pamūjā,
    amwit iṅ aṣṭami kṛṣṇa makaphala rikaṅ swasthāna çrī narendrā.

Canto 84.

Metre: - - ◡ ◡ ◡ ◡ - - - ◡ ◡ ◡ ◡ - - ◡ ◡ ◡ ◡ - ᵕ
20 *feet, a kind of* kṛti.

1. prāptaṅ diwaça khapiṅ pādblas i wijil/ çrī narapati warṇnan,
    tiṅkahnira midĕreṅ nāgara marasuk/ bhūṣana kanakādī,
    çobhābhra pinikul iṅ jampana mahāwan laṇṭaran atuntun,
    mantrī saçiwa bhūjaṅgādinika mañaṅgo dadar iṅiri sök.

2. ghūrṇaṅ paḍata mṛdaṅga trutika duduṅ çāṅka tarayan atrī,
    sinraṅ ni pasĕlur iṅ bhaṭṭagaṇa maṅuccaraṇaṅ abhiwāḍa,
    çlokhastutinira saṅkeṅ parapura de saṅ nipuṇa kawīndrā,
    cihna nṛpati gahan/ lwī raghusuta kṛṣṇañjaya subhageṅ rāt.

3. sāmpun/ nṛpati manek/ riṅ maṇimayā siṅhāsana suminābhra,
    çoḍḍodani sakala lwirnira wahu saṅke jinapada çobhā,
    byakta trisura surendrāṅ umark i himbaṅniran arja hyaṅ,
    āpan/ paḍa linĕwiḥ bhuṣaṇanika sotan waṅ aḍika mu- (129b) lya.

4. tiṅkaḥ ni lakunira çrī nṛpati pajaṅ sapriya pinakagra,
    siṅhāsananira sāmpun/ lpas inarak niṅ balagaṇa kīrṇna,
    mantrī pajaṅ atawā mantri ri paguhan/ rowaṅ ika sapaṇṭa,
    lakṣārwuḍa marasuk/ bhūṣaṇa saha bhṛtya ḍwaja paṭahādī.

5. maṅkā nṛpa ri lasĕm/ sapriya ri wugat/ lampahira sabhṛtya,
    mwaṅ çrī nṛpa ri kaḍintĕn/ sayugala samātya bala ri wuntat saçrī,
    çrī jīwanapurarājñī ri wuri saha bhṛtyagaṇa sabhartta,
    çrī bhūpati pamkas mantry aḍika sayāwawanni mañiri sök.

6. ton taṅ para jana sar sök/ pnuh ariwĕg tanpa sla manonton,
    piṅgir nikanaṅ ḷbuh ajajar taṅ sakatha pinaṅguṅ,
    dwārānapi sawawa lwir ḍwaja ñuniweḥ paṅguṅ ika rinĕṅā,
    sök/ stry anwam atuha dudwaṅ maṅĕbĕk umuṅwiṅ baciṅah
                                                        [atimbun.

7. buddinya daradaran kapwa suka bañun/ wāhuwahu manonton,
   tan warnnan ulah ikeñjiṇ nṛpati kinastryan mijil i wañuntur,
   wiprādi sira maweh amṛta warakuṇdyādi wawan ikāpnĕd,
   mantrī para pamgĕt kapwa maṛk amuṣpañjali paṛñ asraṇ.

———

Canto 85.

Metre: – – – – ᴗ – – – ᴗ ᴗ ᴗ ᴗ ᴗ – – – ᴗ ᴗ ᴗ ᴖ
20 feet, suwadanā.

1. taṅgal niṇ cetra tekaṇ balagaṇa mapuluṇ rahyā (130a) hĕm apupul,
   mantrī mwaṇ taṇda len/ gusti sahana ñuniweḥ wadwā haji tumūt,
   mīlwaṇ mantryākuwu mwaṇ juru buyut athawā wwaṇ riṇ parapurī,
   astam/ saṇ kṣatriya mwaṇ wiku haji karuhun/ sakweḥ dwijawara.

2. doniṇ höman ri tan lamlama ni sabala saṇ çrī nātha riñ ulaḥ,
   kapwānūttājariṇ rāja kapakapa sadāṅkĕn/ cetra winaca,
   haywāñambaḥ ri tan lakwan ika manĕkĕteṇ wastrādyaraṇa,
   dewaswādinya tātan purugĕn ika maran/ swasthāṇ pura sadā.

———

Canto 86.

Metre: – – – – ᴗ ᴗ ᴗ ᴗ – – – ᴗ ᴗ ᴗ – ᴖ
17 feet, mandākrāntā.

1. ākāra rwaṇ dina muwah ikaṇ kāryya kewwan/ narendrā,
   wawwan/ lor niṇ pura tgal anāmaṇ bubat kaprakāça,
   çrī nāthāṅkĕn mara makahawan/ sthāna siñhāpadudwan,
   sabhṛtyānorakn idĕran atyadbhutaṇ wwaṇ manonton.

2. ndan tiṅkaḥniṇ bubat araharārddāratā taṇdĕs alwa,
   madya kroçakaranikan amūrwwānutug/ rājamārgga,
   maddyārddā kroça kta pañalornyānutug piṅgiriṇ lwaḥ,
   kedran deniṇ bhawana kuwuniṇ mantrī sasök mapaṇta.

3. bwatbwat/ muṅgwiṇ tñah aruhur atyadbhutādĕgnya çobhā,
   stambhanyākweh hinukir anathā parwwa tiṅkaḥni- (130b) kāpnĕd,
   skaṇdawāre nikaṭa nika kulwan/ rakĕt lwir pure jro,
   ṅgwan/ çrī nāthan dunuñ i tkaniṇ cetramāsan pamaṅguṇ.

———

Canto 87.

Metre: ⌣ – – – – – ⌣ ⌣ ⌣ ⌣ – – ⌣ ⌣ ⌣ ᵉ
17 feet, çikhariṇī.

1. pratiṅkahniṅ paṅguṅ majajar añalor paçcima muka,
   ri saṇḍiṅ lor mwaṅ dakṣiṇa haji para kṣatriya pinikh,
   sumantrī ḍarmmādyakṣa ktaṅ umarp/ wetan atathā,
   harpnyārddālwā lwir nika saḍawatāniṅ ḷbuh agöṅ.

2. rikā ṅgwan/ çrī nāthan parahita maweḥ netrāwiṣaya,
   hanan/ praṅ taṇḍiṅ praṅ pupuh ikaṅ atembok kanin adu,
   akañjar len prp/ mwaṅ matalitali moghāṅdani ni suka,
   hanan pat/ mwaṅ trī kaṅ dina lawasira çīghran umuliḥ.

3. yyuliḥ çrī nāthekaṅ bubat aspi paṅguṅnya dinawut,
   samaṅkā taṅ praṅ taṇḍiṅ an inura maṅkin/ sukhakara,
   ri paṅlwaṅṅiṅ cetra nṛpatin umiwö çrāma sahana,
   wineḥ wastra mwaṅ bhojana paḍa sukhan mamwit umuliḥ.

Canto 88.

Metre: – ⌣ ⌣ – ⌣ – ⌣ ⌣ ⌣ – ⌣ – ⌣ ⌣ ⌣ – ⌣ – ⌣ ⌣ ⌣ ᵉ
22 feet, madraka.

1. salwir ikaṅ buyut/ wadana teki tan wawaṅ umāntuk amwit i daḷm,
   āryya ranādikāra dinuluniṅ kādipati riṅ eñjiṅ umark,
   āryya mahādikāra juru pañca taṇḍa pinakādi riṅ padlĕgan,
   rowaṅ ikan paḍamwit i sḍaṅ na- (131a) reçwara sirān tinaṅkil
                                                    [apupul.

2. ṅkān pawuwus nareçwara ri wĕṅkĕr ojar i parāndyanādi wadana,
   e khita haywa tan tuhu susatya bhaktyasih aniwyanātha ri hajī,
   sthitya khiteṅ kaweçyan i siṅāṅdane hajĕṅaniṅ pradeça ya gṅĕn,
   setu ḍamarggā waṇḍira gṛhādi salwir ikanaṅ sukīrtti pahayun.

3. mukya nikaṅ gagā sawah asiṅ tinandur iṅ kawṛḍḍya rakṣan amĕrṇ,
   yāwat ikaṅ lmaḥ pinakarāmakĕn/ pagĕha tanpa dadya waluha,
   hetu nikaṅ kulīna tan atuṇḍuṅeṅ amaradeça yan patarukā,
   naṅ pratiguṇḍalanya ya tutĕn/ ri göṅanikanaṅ pradeçan uṣiṛn.

4. çrī krtawarddaneçwara hamaywanī kagĕnan iŋ pradeça gawayĕn,
ndan wilanĕn mahānasār ikan pramādanika riŋ pjah çaçi sāda,
milwa ta yomapeksa hananiŋ durātmaka makādyañidra lawana,
wrddyani drwya sang prabhū phalanya sādananirān/ rumaksa
[bhuwana.

5. çrī nrpa tiktawilwanāgareçwarānupasaman sumintĕn amuwus,
sāmya naranya rakwa kadadinya teki katkanya haywa wisamma,
yan hana rājakāryya palawaŋ makadi nika tan hanan/ nĮwata,
yan pa- *(131b)* sgĕh muwah wruhanahā swadehanika sāmyalaksaṇa
[gĕgĕn.

Canto 89.

Metre: – ◡ ◡ – – ◡ ◡ – – ◡ ◡ ◡ ◡ ◡ – ◡ ◡ – ◡ ◡ ℗
20 feet, a kind of krti.

1. mwaŋ rasaniŋ pratiguṇḍala panadĕgirebu hajīka tutĕn,
eñjina yan paḍananratnana sabhinuktinikān pasgĕh,
yan hana mūrkka tikaŋ sin-gĕhan agawe lara sāhasikā,
tūt sasinambat ikā sinawakanika tājarakĕn/ ri kami.

2. āpan ikaŋ pura len/ swawisaya sinhā lawan gahana,
yan/ rusakaŋ thani milwan akuran upajiwa tikaŋ nāgara,
yan taya bhrtya katon wayanīka para nūsa tkānrwĕkā,
etunikān/ paḍa raksan apagĕha kalih phalaniŋ mawuwus.

3. nāhan ujarnira riŋ para wadana sahur nika sapraṇata,
eka hatur nika tan/ salah anuta saliŋ naranātha kabeh,
mantry upapattyanananěkal athaca para handyan ateki mark,
thog tumibān ghaṭita traya panaḍahireky apupul caritan.

4. uttarapūrwwa witanna kahananira çobha rinanga huwus,
riŋ tri witāna matūt/ padu mara wadanādyapupul/ tinatā,
prāpta tika taḍah uttama wawan ika sarwwa suwarṇṇamaya,
çīghra tika humarp/ harpakn atitah ri harp/ nrpati.

5. lwirni *(132a)* taḍahnira mesa mahisa wihaga mrga wök/ maḍupā,
mīna lawan tikañ aṇḍah ajarin aji lokapurāṇa tinūt,
çwāna kara krimi mūsika hilahila len/ wiyuŋ nalpa dahat,
çatrw awamāna hurip/ ksaya cala nika rakwa yadi purugĕn.

Canto 90.

Metre: – – – ⌣ ⌣ ⌣ ⌣ – ⌣ – – ⌣ – ͝
13 feet, praharṣiṇī.

1. prāptaŋ bhojana makadon rikaŋ wwañ akweḥ,
   sañkĕp sarwwarājatha bhojananya çobhā,
   matsyāsañkya sahana riŋ darat/ mwañ i wwai,
   rāprp/ drāk/ rumawuh anūt kramānuwartta.

2. maṇḍūka krimi kara mūṣika çṛgāla,
   kweḥ çakterika winahan tamaḥnya tuṣṭa,
   deni wwaŋ nika dudu riŋ sadeçadeça,
   sāmbĕknyeki tinuwukhan/ dumeḥ ya tuṣṭā.

3. lwir niŋ pāna surasa tan/ pgat mawantu,
   twak nyu twak/ çiwalan/ harak hano kilaŋ bṛm,
   mwaŋ tampo siñ aḍika taŋ hane harp/ sök,
   sarwwā mās/ wawan ika dudw anekawarṇna.

4. rombeḥ mwaŋ guci tikanaŋ prakīrṇna lumrā,
   arḍḍākweḥ sajĕñ ika dātwanekawarṇna,
   tanpantyaŋ larih aliwĕr bañun way adṛs,
   sāmbĕknyāñgapan umutaḥ waneḥ byamoha.

5. praḥpraḥ nṛpatin aweḥ khasukan/ pamukti,
   yan waŋ çakta pa- (132b) ḍa pinarān/ larihnya limpad,
   tan dadyāmiḍi riñ alaḥ tlas kasĕñkwan,
   riŋ wwaŋ māna lagi wĕṛwĕṛ ginuywan.

6. rāmyaŋ gitada pañiduŋ nikān maganti,
   kīrtti çrī nṛpati linañwakĕnyan añras,
   mañkin tuṣṭa sañ añinūm/ samenake twas,
   sowenyālaha wkasan maguywaguywan.

———

Canto 91.

Metre: – ᵛ ᵛ – ᵛ – ᵛ ᵛ ᵛ – ᵛ ᵛ ᵛ ᵛ ᵛ ⏑
17 feet, wamçapatrapatita.

1. jurwiyaṅin/ cucud sahā buyūt nikan amacĕḥ macĕḥ,
   prāpta manṛtta riŋ çwaran umāmbil i sadulur ikā,
   solahulaḥ nikāmuhara guyw anukani lumihat,
   etunikhān wineḥ waçaṇa taŋ para wadana kabeḥ.

2. ri wkasan kinon/ maṛka milwalariha ri haṛp,
   mantry upapatti kapwa dinulurnyan alariḥ aṅiduŋ,
   maṅhuri khaṇḍamohi paṅiduŋnira titir inalm,
   çrī nṛpatin widagḍa manulaṅgapi ṛsp alaṅö.

3. gīta narendrā maŋhlahlāṅdani jñĕr aṅanī,
   mrak mañawuwwaṅ i padapa tulyanika riṅ alaṅö,
   lwir mmaḍu len/ guladrawa rinok/ riṅ amanis añĕñĕr,
   waṅça maghāṣa tulyanika riṅ ṛs aṅuṅĕr i hati.

4. hāryya raṇāḍikāra lali yan hatur i narapati,
   hāryya mahāḍikāra ta dulur nika paṛṅ amuwus,
   ān/ para handyan āpti miha- *(133a)* te siran arakhĕrakhĕt,
   ā juga liṅnirā t-hĕr umāntuk/ hadadadakan.

5. çrī kṛtawarddaneçwara mamañjaki sira rumuhun,
   ṅkāna rika witāna ri tṅaḥ rinacana dinadak,
   çorinireki gitada lawan/ tkĕsira rahajöŋ,
   sotan ulaḥ karāmyan ikanaŋ guyu juga winaṅun.

6. ndāluwaran sireki ri dataŋ narapatin aṅadĕg,
   gītanirānyat aṅdani gīrahyasĕn iṅ umulat,
   çoranireki suçrama nirukti lituhayu wagĕd,
   gita nikāṅhiribhirib aweḥ ṛsĕpaniṅ umulat.

7. çrī naranātha tan sipi wagusnira tlas arasuk,
   aṣṭa tkĕsnirekin upabhāryya rahayu sawala,
   tusniṅ amatya waṅça wicakṣaṇa tĕtĕs iṅ ulaḥ,
   etunirān pabañwal anibākĕn ucapan aṅne.

8. naŋ nawanātya kapwa tinapaknira tinĕwĕkakĕn,
     asya makādi tan pat ikaŋ guyu paṛṅ aslur,
     mwaŋ karuṇāmaṅun taṅis aweḥ skĕl apuhara luḥ,
     etu nikaŋ tumon/ paḍa kamānuṣan aṅĕnaṅĕn.

9. siṅhitiṅ ārkka liṅsir irika nṛpatin atlasan,
     ṅkā para handyan amwit umusap/ ri padatala hajī,
     liŋ nika muktapāpa sinuṅan sukha kadi tan i rāt,
     tan/ wuwusĕn/ stuti- (*133b*) nya haji sampun umuliḥ hi daḷm.

CHAPTER 15 - CONCLUSION.

Canto 92.

Metre: - - - ◡ ◡ - ◡ - ◡ ◡ ◡ - ◡ ◡ ◡ ◡ ◡ - - ◡ - ◡ ꝑ
23 feet, jagaddhita.

1. maṅkā tiṅkahirān/ pamukti sukha riṅ pura tumkani seṣṭiniṅ manaḥ,
tātaḥhan lara dahat/ ndatan malupa riṅ kaparahitan i haywaniṅ
[prajā,
ānwam/ tapwana kabwatan sira tathāpi sugata sakalān/
[mahārddikā,
deniṅ jñāna wiçeṣa çūdda pamaḍĕmnira ri kuhakaniṅ durātmaka.

2. ndātan mahuwusan kawīryyanira len/ wibhawanira dudūg/ riṅ
[ambarā,
siṅgiḥ çrī girināthamūrtti makhajanma ri siran agawe jagadditā,
byāktā maṅguh upadrawāwihaṅ i sājñanira manasar iṅ samāhitā,
moktaṅ kleça kĕta katona ṅuniweḥ wuwusana tika saṅ sadā mark.

3. nāhan hetuni kottamān/ nṛpati kaprakāçitaṅ pinujīṅ jagattraya,
sakweḥniṅ jana maḍyamottama kaniṣṭa paḍa mujarakĕn/
[çwarāstutī,
aṅhiṅ sotnika mogha laṅgĕṅ atuwuḥ wukira sira paṅöbaniṅ sarāt,
astwānīrwa lawas/ bhaṭāra rawicandrama sumĕḷh i bhūmimāṇḍala.

Canto 93.

Metre: - - - - ◡ .. -- - ◡ ◡ ◡ ◡ ◡ - - - ◡ - - - ◡ ꝑ
21 feet, sragdharā.

1. sakweḥ saṅ paṇḍitaṅ anyaḍarani maṅikĕt kāstawan/ çrī narendrā,
çrī buddādity saṅ bhikṣwagaway i sira bhogawwali (*134a*) çloka
[kīrṇṇa,
riṅ jambudwīpa toṅwānira maṅaran i kañcipurī ṣadwihāra,
mwaṅ saṅ wiprāṅaran/ çrī mutali sahṛdayāwat/ stuti çloka çūdda.

2. astam/ saŋ paṇḍiteŋ bhūmi jawa saha saŋ çāstradakṣātiwijña,
kapwāgostyāṅikĕt/ çloka hana wacawacan/ ṅgwānirekin pamārṇna,
mukyā muṅgwiŋ praçāsti stuti nṛpati tkap/ saŋ suḍarmmopapatti,
saŋ wruḥ riṅ gita gitenikĕtiran aṅikĕt/ stotra lumreŋ purī jro.

Canto 94.

Metre: - - - ◡ ◡ - - ◡ - ◡ ◡ ◡ - ◡ ◡ ◡ ◡ ◡ ◡ - - - ◡ ◡ ∞
23 feet, jagaddhita.

1. āmbĕk saŋ maparāb/ prapañca kapitūt/ mihat i parakawīçwareŋ
[purā,
mīlwāmarṇna ri kastawanṛpati dūra paṅikt ika lumra riŋ sabhā,
aṅhiŋ stutya ri jöŋ bhaṭāra girinātha patnanika mogha sanmatan,
tan len/ prārtthana haywaniŋ bhuwana mukya ri pagĕha narendrā
[riŋ prajā.

2. riŋ çākadri gajāryyamāçwayujamāsa çubhadiwaça pūrṇnacandrama,
ṅkā hīngan/ rakawin/ pamarṇnana khadigwijayanira narendrā
[riŋ prajā,
kweḥniṅ deça riniñci donika minustaka maṅarana deçawarṇnana,
paṅgil/ paṅhwata sanmata nṛpati mengĕta riṅ alawas ātpadeŋ laṅö.

3. nirwyā teki lawasnira çriṅ aṅikĕt/ kakawin awtu bhāsa riŋ karas,
tĕmbeyanya çā- (*134b*) kābda piṅrwanika lambaṅ i tlas ika parwwa
[sāgara,
nāhan teki catūrtthi bhiṣmaçaraṇantya nika sugataparwwa
[warṇnana.
lāmbaŋ mwaŋ çakakāla taŋ winaluyan gatinikan amĕwĕḥ turuŋ pgat.

4. donyān maṅkana wṛḍḍya yan paṅikĕte haji kathamapi tan tame
[laṅö,
göŋ bhāktyāsih anātha hetunikapakṣa tumuta saṅ umāstawe hajī,
çlokā mwaṅ kakawin kiduŋ stuti nike haji makamuka deçawarṇnana,
ṅhiŋ tohnyeki wilājja niçcaya yadin guyuguyun apa deya lāmpunĕn.

Canto 95.

Metre: ˘ ˘ ˘ ˘ − ˘ − ˘ ˘ ˘ − ˘ ˘ ˘ ˘ ˘ ˘ ⌀
18 feet, a kind of dhṛti.

1. purih iṅ awan/ lanenaḷh iṅ adyah akikuk i ḍusun,
   aṛtu kuraŋ prahāsana kumul kuna riṅ ujar arūm,
   dugaduga sātya sāḍu juga sih lalis ika matilar,
   mapa karikāpa don wruh ika riŋ smarawiḍi wiphalā.

2. karaṇanikānapih wiṣaya tan/ karaktan iṅ ulah,
   wuta tuli tan/ wru lagrinīnaḷh niṅ alara katilar,
   pawarawarah mahāmuni dudūga rin-gĕp i hati,
   pijĕr aṅiwö kriyādwaya mataṅya tan umur atilar.

3. Ịkas ika tan/ pahi mwaṅ atapeṅ giriwana manusup,
   agaway umah pahoman asnöt/ jnĕk amati tutur,
   kamala na- *(135a)* tarnya len asana tanduran ika maruhur,
   kamalasana ywa nāma ni sāmpun alawas amatĕk.

———

Canto 96.

Metre: ˘ − − ˘ ˘ − − ⌀ / ⌀ ˘ − − ˘ − ˘ ⌀
8 + 8 feet, wipulāwaktra.

1. prapañca pracacah pañca, pracacad/ pocapan/ cĕcĕd,
   prapöŋpöŋ pipi pucce pṛm, pracoŋcoŋ cĕt pacĕhpacĕh.

2. tan/ tata tīta tan tutĕn, tan tĕtĕs/ tan tut iŋ tutur,
   titik/ tantrī tateŋ tatwa, tutun/ tāmtām/ titir ttitih.

———

Canto 97.

Metre: ˘ ˘ − ˘ ˘ − − ⌀ / ⌀ − − ˘ ˘ − ˘ ˘
8 + 8 feet, wipulāwaktra.

1. samalān/ pu winādāprih, prih dānā wipulān/ masa,
   tāmā san/ çara riŋ gatyā, tyāga riŋ rasa sanmatā.

2. yaçā saŋ winadānuṅsī, sinuŋ dāna wisañçaya,
   yan aweh magawe tibra, bratī wega maweḥ naya.

3. mataruŋ tuhu wānyapraŋ, praŋnya waḥhu turuŋ tama,
   masa liṅgara çūnya priḥ, priḥnya çūra galiŋ sama.

———————

Canto 98.

Metre: – – ⌣ ⌣ ⌣ ⌣ ⌣ ⌣ – ⌣ – ⌣ ⌣ ⌣ – ⌣ ⌣ ⌣ ⌣ ⌣ ⌣ ⊖
22 feet, a kind of wikṛti.

1. yan bwat para kawi maparab/ winādan atapa brata kṛta juga
                                                    [rin-gĕp,
   maitryāsih iṅ alulut upekṣa riŋ huwus awarsih ariris iṅ ulaḥ,
   tyāge sukha wibhawa yatan katĕmwa sakahananika nukhani saphalā,
   tātan huniṅa mihat i solahiŋ para wināda cinala ri ni daḷm.

———————

NĀGARA-KĔRTĀGAMA COLOPHONS.

Ms. Or. Leyden University Library 5023, p. 135.

Colophon I.

Itī nāgarakṛtāgama samāpta, saṅkatha çrī mahārāja wilwātikta, (135b) tkeŋ nuṣa pranuṣā kacayeŋ sira, makādi bālīrājya pratiṣṭāṅkana, makānimitaŋ saŋhyaŋ praçāsti waçītā, tkeŋ yawadwīpa samantā.

Colophon II.

Samaṅkana tlas tinular, tkāpnirārcapamāsah, ṅkāneŋ khañcānasthāna, hiŋ pulina bālī, riŋ thānī pradeça kawyān/ riŋ wetān iŋ talaga dwāja, sḍĕṅiŋ tinaṅguŋ rīpu, kuraŋ kawotnya kapayuṅā de saŋ lotātī çṛḍḍā māccha, āpan tan tameŋ guru laghū pasaṅān, hakeḥ prabheḍanyā, kewalwya milwa matraŋ nurāt, riŋ dinā, u, wṛ, khiraṅgāpahaŋ; kārttikha māsaniŋ paniḷmān, i çāka, pakṣaŋ ṛṅö ghanā dewa, 1662; samana kowusanya sinurāt, kāmpuraha dyanira saŋ manĕmwaŋ dlāha makadi saṅ amāccha, dumadyāknaŋ kadirghāyūṣanira saṅ anurat, oṃ dirghāyūr astu tatāstu hastu, auṃ sāmasāmpūrṇnaya nāmaḥ swāhā.

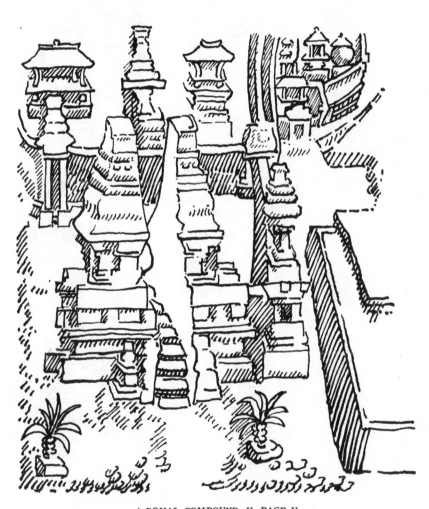

A ROYAL COMPOUND, V. PAGE V.

MINOR WRITINGS

TEXTS

NAWANATYA

according to Ms. Or. Leyden 5091, p. 1a—24a.

SELECTIONS.

(1a) // o // awīghnam āstu // o // nihan hawanattya, kawruhakna de saŋ mahyun āṅambaha rājya, hapan yan hanaha wwaŋ tan/ wruha riŋ nawanatya, tan yogya wehana ṅambaha sajroniŋ paṅastryan, iṅanana sayawiniṅ alunālun, maŋkana lwiriṅ āyun āṅambaha rājya, tan wruha riŋ hawanatya, nāgarakramā rājyawasanā pañcawisaya, nawanatya jabā riŋ jro/ ikā lwirnya, mapa prayoganya, ikā nawanatya, ndi lwirnya, hulahniŋ maçawītā, hamet riṅariṅa, hanuju smitā, tkapniŋ saŋ mahyun āsawitā// iti nawanatya sawitā, hulahaknā, mṛga, mātsyā, paṇa, dyuta, çṛṅgara, haṣya, samara, çrama, kalaṅĕn, (1b)

(2b) // mapa çramā, yan saŋ ratu lumkās haçramāçramā riŋ maṅuntur, aywa tan wruḥ (3a) phalayuniŋ saŋ ratu, malayu makādi dṛtta, hanāmbantala, hana ppuṣpākajaya, hana liṅaphala, han paṅkaja nawaŋ, muwaḥ dṛta, hana hlĕtlĕt, hana kājog, wuwusanan, maŋkana sikĕpantā haywā pilih, sikĕp, kaŋ prayoga phalaywākna, raṅin, galaḥ, buntal tameṅ, hikū prayogakna lawan halpniŋ phalayu, ika yogya, hulahulahakna, de saŋ mahyun asawītā, donya magaweya pāṅlahlaniŋ saŋ çīnawītā/ muwaḥ kalaṅwan, yan saŋ ratu lumkās āndon kalaṅwan, hana tārumniŋ pasir wūkīr, hana mṅaṅana bhaṣa, hamrayogakna tamantamanan, wūkīrwūkīran, pājöŋpajĕŋṅan, den kadi ha (3b) nmu skār sawaṇa, pilih i gāṇḍanya, mwaŋ warṇnanyā, phalanya magawayakĕn sihniŋ saŋ çīnawītā, ika ta hulahulahĕn de saŋ mahyun sumawītā, manūt i kārṣa saŋ prabhū, ndan īnāran mantri mūkya, hapatih amaṅku bhūmi, dyakṣa haṅku kaprabhun, ikā pinakamukyāniŋ rajyā, pinakaguṇaniŋ rakryan āpatih, riŋ jabā riŋ jro, makaṅūnī laṅlaṅiŋ bhūmī, hamañca nāgara, wruḥ riŋ sarwwa bhaṣa, sarwwa haṣtra, sarwwāgama, wiḍagḍa, wira, wiweka, prajña, pragiwakā, sarwwāyuddā, wruḥ riŋ

6

don, mwaŋ donyā kīrakīra, samā, hupayā, samahitta, parahitta, mañu-
lusi droŋ rodra, lagaweŋñārtthā, tan ajriḥ riŋ lokīkā, paramārtthā,
tutugiŋ guṇa, (4a) pinakakāhot iŋ salagan, de saŋ prabhū, yan hana
wwaŋ maṅkana, ikā guṇanya, wnaŋ dadyākna hapatih amaṅku bhūmi //
iti guṇaniŋ rakryan āpatiḥ, sami waṅça sakamakāmā, wnaŋ miçeṣā hiŋ
sanāgara, tinuwatuwā riṅ mantrī, wnaŋ hañurip āmatyani wadwa saha-
çra, wahanā wnaŋ sakamakamā, hajoñ jnar, ḍampa rakta, pawahan
kañcanā, wnaŋ hiniriŋ tabĕhtabĕhan, wnaŋ sinambah iŋ çabhā, wnaŋ
wahana muṅgwiŋ pañāstryan, iti nugrahā kapātihan// guṇanirā mpu
dyakṣā, wruh aṅupacaranī kaprabhūn, wnaŋ haniṅkaḥ çarīranira saŋ
prabhū, hamrayogyakakĕn kayogyan, haṅruraḥ glĕglĕh iŋ purā, aṅā-
stityakĕna sarwwa huta (4b) ma, ambĕnĕrākĕn mariŋ kanītiyoghyan,
hasuŋ marggā pāḍan, halṅkara wr̥tti, kawr̥dihaniŋ kaprabhūn, wkasan-
iŋ guṇa, wruhiŋ sarwwa mūkya, iti guṇa kaçewan // nugrahanya,
hatiṅkaḥ saŋ paṇḍita rajya, deçanya sakalagyaniŋ bhūmi jawa, wadwanya hahiṅana pamariwr̥tā, sakayakaya, makādi hapawohan ākanaka,
ḍampa wuluŋ, jöŋ wuluŋ, wnaŋ wahana muṅgwiŋ pañāstryan, wnaŋ
sinĕmbah iŋ sabhā, wnaŋ hañambaḥ kaŋ tan bara, wnaŋ tanpalarapan,
iti nugraha kaçewan.

(5a) // o // kaṅ hiṅāran hawanatya, yen papuphulan, mwaŋ rāja waṇa
ratu, mantrī guru, dwījā, çabhā, sadya, kaka, hari mwaŋ paṇḍitā, haḍḍi,
ikā ta makapamtuniŋ nawanātya, mapa lwirnya, yan hanā wwaŋ tan
wruheriya, kadyāṅganiŋ kr̥mī tan manon, yan wruherīka, sarūmniŋ
kusumā sawarṇna, wilaṅĕn gaṇḍanya, wyaktīka kawaça, donya wnaŋ
pinakatuladiṅ āhurip, phalanya tan hana sameriya, ndi prayoganya,
nawa ṅaraniŋ sasaṅā, natya ṅaraniŋ smītā, ikaŋ smītā sakamakamā
gnĕpaneriya, smita pamtuniŋ pariyaya . . . .

(7b) // hana yogya siṅgahana de saŋ hanĕŋ rajyā, makādi saṅ āsawitā,
pañcawiṣaya, ṅaranya, ndi ta lwirnya, ganda, çwara, rūpā, sparṣā, raṣa.

(9a) // muwaḥ yoga ana keñötākna tatāniṅ nāgara ṅaranya, ndi hiṅaran
agara sakawtu, tanpa ñliwati pasawaçawahan, ndi purā, sajroniŋ bale
baŋ, ndi pöhniŋ puri, sajroniŋ pañastryan // muwaḥ tatā mantrī,
katrīṇi, hino, sirikan, halu, muwah amañcanāgara, patiḥ, tumĕṅguŋ,
dmuŋ, kanuruhan, juru pañālasan, hanlaniŋ wūriniŋ tumĕṅguŋ, juru
pañālasan i (9b) ṅaran, panewon, kālihblaḥ, ṅa, satusekĕt, muwaḥ

mantri dalĕm, hanlani, kaliwon, wage, pon, pahiŋ, manis, sapuluh arĕp
iŋ dmuŋ, kāryya mantri, rakryyan tumĕnguŋ, çiniwi wani, giṇa, klar,
prakāça, warṇnāñjrihi, aprabhā, bhiramā, lagaweŋ nartthā, kinalulutan
deniŋ mantrī, kāryyānraksa pitñĕn saŋ prabhū, raja laranan, raja kapakapa, hanalapi harusuh, kaḷnkaniŋ bhūmī, hanraksa pasar, wolunewu
sadinā sakiŋ pasar, paranira rakryyan tumĕnguŋ, deça wit katumĕngu-
nan, patanewu deça//para marin anabehiŋ taṇḍā wado hajī, lilimā, pari-
çraha lilimā, wadwa hahinan, nĕm atus, wusniŋ tumĕnguŋ paŋlsuŋ,
tumrap (10a) āryyādikāra, sor akryyan tumĕnguŋ, mapan wus tumĕnguŋ // rakryyan dĕmaŋ guṇanya, hamoŋ hanupacara saŋ prabhū,
salwirin agawe tuwī sukā// ndi ta rakryyan dmuŋ tinkahnya, hamon iŋ
saptāçwara, gitā nṛta, pajönpajönan, makanūni pamimimban, mwaŋ
byuha kalanwan, pacankraman, anrupaka kāwibhawan, mwaŋ panange,
hanāthanātha kāraçmin, rarasiŋ çrngarā, kāwyakāraṇa, salwiriŋ gamlan,
makanūni salukat, samahepā, mṛdanga, pasamuhaniŋ strī, tawahaniŋ
taṇḍa daḷm, mwaŋ taṇḍa wan, rūmniŋ ringitan, triguṇā, hamarṇna-
mārṇna rarasniŋ strī riŋ purī, lyaniŋ daḷm, tkeŋ yawī, mwaŋ paburwan-
burwan, pamicakuran, ramyaniŋ pamimimba (10b) n, hawe sukāniŋ
strī, mankana guna rakryyan dmuŋ, yan āna wwaŋ mankana, guṇanya,
wnaŋ jumnĕna dmuŋ, wīryyanya, wnaŋ hamiçesa, hiŋ tutunganan,
wahananiŋ saŋ prabhū tuwi wnaŋ hanangeha sabhūsaṇa, tan hana
hamikalperiya, wadwanya hatisanan, tiganatus, deça wit kadmunan,
sewu deça, dma kālihewu sadinā, balabur sakiŋ daḷm, hupacaranya,
wnaŋ sapcakiŋ hasṭa // guṇa rakryan kanuruhan, hatinkah lingihiŋ saŋ
mantrī, kala wijilwijilan, mwaŋ tātha bhyūhaniŋ natūran, hapeksā
gunlitniŋ wijilan, saprabeya, hatinkah ayĕnan, harākan, kala kawolu,
galanan, wariga, sançana (11a) n, panapitu, tan liwat iŋ sira rakryyan
kanuruhan, mapa lwirniŋ kawolu, rakryyan kanuruhan, hatungu dinā
ratrī, sinawitā riŋ sarwwakrīya, tikĕltikĕlan, sinhasānā, panguŋ çwetā,
tankĕban, lantaran, hamparan, dadardadaran, riŋ yawi mwaŋ riŋ daḷm,
hatinkah wiwijilan, tan āgya mijil suŋ saŋ prabhū, yan tan rakryyan
kanuruhan daṭĕŋ riŋ jro daḷm hanaturi, tkeŋ yawi hatinkah abawaba-
wahan, hamilih patĕhpatĕhan, matinkah strī manimbanī, lantāy mahuḷs
rakta, jon kuniŋ, na, pawohan kañcanā, na, kinaçwanī, hiliran kanakā,
na, sāma kana (11b) n, kerin, samaran çwetā rakta, na, curiga kapra-
wīran mungwiŋ hārṣā, paṛk lan san iŋ daḷm, tan hanā strī mambawani,
samarasa, gumanti ḍampa saŋ prabhū saha garini, pinajĕnan, wuluniŋ
mañurā, habubunkul kañcanā, antyanta subaga rakryyan kanuruhan,
hapĕpĕk salwiriŋ mantrī, habasahan mawḍiyan, ṣaha joŋ, saha nugrahā,
tan madoh lawan jampaṇā, saŋ prabhū katirāmeniŋ sinhāçaṇā, rakryyan

kanuruhan hatiṅkaḥ strī maṅimbaṅi, wus maṅkana, saṅ dwījā maçanti,
saha wweḍa gaṇṭaghaṇṭi, wus maṅkana, rakryyan kanuruhan hamuṣpā
riṅ saṅ prabhū, sawusira saṅ prabhū mareṅārṣa hajnar āṣṭa, haṅlugu-
hakĕn skār ura (12a), rasarasa ṅa, paliṅgih ārūpit, wus maṅkana, t-hĕr
mayĕṅ rakryyan kanuruhan lumakwiṅ ṅārṣa, anā giliṅan, ragas, saṅ
mantrī samā keçaḍarā, saṅ āwṛḍā, samā ragas, walinin arakāṇ ḍatĕṅ
pṛṣṭaniṅūnī, rakryyan kanuruhan haṅlud i paṅabhaktya, turunaniṅ
siṅhāçaṇā, maṅkana ta tiṅkaḥ de rakryyan kanuruhan, gamanti saṅsaṅan
sami lawan galaṅan, pahenya tar añjabā, sama paniṅkah rakryyan kanuruhan, muwah guṇā mukyā, sasaraniṅ wwaṅ nuṣantara, yan kala
maṅajawa, sakecayeṅ yawī, tan lyan rakryyan kanuruhan, hikāṅ
amaṅgihi sopacarā, makādi bhūktyānya, sakār (12b) pnya, bhaṣanya
sakārp salwir bhaṣa, kaṅ wruḥ rakryyan kanuruhan, haṅūlahi buḍḍi
hapuṅkwas, wani kalahiṅ ṅārttha, mwaṅ labda, aṅacarani ḍatĕṅanira
saṅ prabhū, yekā guṇa rakryyan kanuruhan, ikāṅ amaṅgihi sopacara,
winawanya sakerīya, sama wadwā lawan rakryyan dĕmuṅ, mwaṅ para
sakiṅ daḷm // guṇa rakryyan raṅga, anūt kawiran saṅ prabhū, widagḍa
riṅ pasasaraman, wruh iṅ sarwwa yudḍa, sarwwa sañjata, sawarṇna-
warṇnaniṅ saṇḍaṅsaṇḍaṅan, wruh aprayoga, kna sikĕp, hanor tāsor
paṅaḷmiṅ ḷwihiṅ wadwa saṅ prabhū, tar yogya wehĕn saṇḍaṅsaṇḍaṅan,
nugahaniṅ wīro riṅ (13a) praṅ, yan waṅ maga wataṅ wireriya, nugrahanya siṅĕl, wataṅ jinijriṅ, yan waṅ āḍaḍap, patitiḥ rahī, kalambi
sinimpisimpiṅ, hambuluṅan, ḍaḍap iṅĕmasan, twĕk malelā, hiṅĕmasan,
yan waṅṅ ābuntal ātameṅ, wīrerīya, nugrahanya, susuṅkul, tampak
wāja, garuḍa marp, tameṅ sinawatareṅ kañcanā, buntal ācamara, ika
ta mtu sakeṅ rakryyan raṅgā, guṇa mūkya, yan sa prabhū, malayu
riṅ maṅuntur, tan lyan kaṅ pār phayunira, makādi pūḍĕtānira, tansaḥ
pinakaraṅga, tkaniṅ praṅ, towī, gawyakĕn, wot muṅgwiṅ bhaya, kālaniṅ
parupūtiṅ kewĕh // iti guṇa mantrī tiga, ti (13b) ga guṇānira yya
lāṅkā, bhīçekāṅūjar, hamarwa matigāndikānira saṅ prabhū, haṅūpacarā
labda mwaṅ çāstra, kaṅ mewĕh, tuwāgaṇā riṅ çāstrā, ahiṅan wīryyanu-
pābhara de saṅ prabhū // kāryya rakryyan juru paṅalasan, hinuṅsi
deniṅ saṅ mahyun hasawitā, tan patipati yan tan hawit iṅ juru paṅalasan, hiṅaran, yan āna wwaṅ mahyun āsawitā, tār agya paṛkākna,
pisĕsĕgĕn sawulan, sahekanya, awā kweh kriya hupayaniṅ musuḥ, ḷupūt
pinisĕsĕg, warahana kāryyaniṅ nāgarā, wus pwa sirā, lumakwā sĕm-
bahna riṅ saṅ prabhū, rakryyan juru paṅalasan, panaṅkaniṅ paṅupakā
(14a) ra, cumpuha bhūktinya bhūṣaṇanya, wus tĕkah pasawitanya,
rakryyan juru paṅalasan āmayakna, sadĕmaknya, maṅkanā kramāniṅ
juru paṅalasan // makaguṇa haṅacarani donan, sireṅ dwīdaça bhalya

pinakayakanira saŋ rowlas bale, ndi haran rowlas bale, pañada, tañjuŋ, groṅgro, pagĕmpuran, jayanāgara, tanpalwir, çubhanimitā, tamtaman, suminaŋ, nyūgaḍiŋ, rājadewī, sumambiŋ, gnĕp rowlas bale, hari yan hanā don, rakryyan juru pañalasan hatiṅkah iriya, sārīsārīniŋ batur, sinlir, rajaça, wado hyaŋ, çiwiçiwiniŋ hyaŋ // muwaḥ wiṣnuwaddaṇā, tansaḥ dinā ra *(14b)* trī hamawa pahidwan, kāryyanya, sinlir, siniwisiwi, tumuṇḍa wiraghatha wiratanu sosoraniŋ woŋ wiṣṇuwarḍḍanā, haṅupacara reḥ juru rakryyan pañalasan // muwaḥ kāryya dūta kawruhakna, ...

(17b) // muwaḥ tata purā kawruhakna, mapa lwirniŋ tata purā, tatkālaniŋ mijil, haṅraṅsuk mahābhūṣaṇa, sakṣat teja saŋ hyaŋ haditya snĕnira, paliṅihan amparan, sahā pramaḍani kasurkasuran, mwaŋ pataraṇa, hamlĕk gandaniŋ dupā, hiŋ çabhā, liṅsir kunaṅ, hulapulap, huñcalhuñcal *(18a)*, tuwi tumamā sirerika, baktabaktan, sahesira, pahidwan kanaka, patoyan mabhūṣaṇa, kpĕt saha camara, joṅ muṅguh irikā, curiga, sakāmakama, haliṅih tā pwa sira, hapatĕh haṅliṅani puṣpa, tan owah apaçilan, wūlatira tanāna kālīwatan, wruh iŋ naya, phalarpharan towī, ndi wnaŋ sinaṅguh phalarphalaran, wkawkaniŋ sureŋ praŋ, wkawka suçīlā, prajñaṇa, mantrī magulaŋgulaŋ, saha saŋsiptā, prayoga, guṇa, prajña wiweka, wnaŋ magulaṅgulaŋ, parananiṅ andikā, mantryāmañcanāgara, pataŋ ḍpā dohanya maliṅgih, saha hupacarā, mantrī katrīnī, riŋ wūri sadeṅiriṅan, mantrī wṛdaḥ, tan ādoh *(18b)* pataryan haji hikā, ndi mantrī wṛdah, çenapatiḥ, haryyādikāra, wiraradya hikā mantri wṛdaḥ, mantri bhūjaṅga tigaŋ dpa dohanya, saŋ brahmāna purohita, reñcaṅan tāliṅih, muṅwiŋ harṣā, haṇḍapa sahaṅguli sakeŋ sirā, mantri bhūjaṅgā, sahati haṇḍapanya, len sakeŋ sirā, sakawnaŋwnaŋ, muwah pilī ṅandikā, tan maçriṅa, tan mnĕña, ...

// *(21b)* // hana wadwa hatuwa, tanpa carāywa dūrçīlā, lobhā, çakteŋ wiṣayetama, tan pūrṇna, hikā tan yogyā ṅgonĕn de saŋ mahyun wadwā, makādi saŋ suja *(22a)* nma, saŋ ratu tuwi tan wadwaha ikā, magawe heñaniŋ wadwa, tan tuhuniŋ wadwa mulāt, çīlāniŋ janma wṛḍḍā yan maṅkanā, yan asaṅādi hagawe, pacarāniŋ manaḥ, hatawi sapocapana, hagawe prakāmpaniŋ çīla, yaktī haloṅ kaputut iŋ çīla mankanā, rehnya hatuwa çīla maṅkana, saksat maṅuṅkuli puriṣa sajamban, yan sapocapana lan janma maṅkana, rehnya tuwa // hana janma susatya, prajña suçīla, wīra tuwī, wīweka, mawḍiŋ lokikā, hawṛḍḍah tuwuḥnya, saḍū, ikā ta yan ana wwaŋ maṅkana, gulaṅ alunĕn rehana henak āmbĕk, yata ḍanā, tansah agunitaha lawan wadwā, salwir phalarphalaran, *(22b)*

ṅgonanyā tañataña, malar katṛhana salaḥ saçīki çīlānya // muwaḥ
deniṅ amṛnaḥ wadwa jějěriḥ, muwaḥ saḍū, pṛnaḥnyā ṅūliliṅiṅ wěṅku-
niṅ purī, salisiṛn, phalanya, waṅ jějěriḥ yan pinakapikāndělan, yatna
haṅgugoni katakutan, tanpasuṅ yan ana rusakāniṅ lalayan, deniṅ
wḍinya, maṅkanaḍu, tan lupteṅ rarakṣanya, jriḥnya manawa hala
sakerīyā, hikā dibyanya, // hikaṅ waṅ wana lawan marusuḥ, pṛnahanyā,
jabaniṅ nagarā, haṅrakṣaha saṅ ana riṅ jro, pamamāṅanya deça niṅ
musuḥ, ḍatěṅa riṅ jro puraniṅ musuḥ, paṅrurusuhanya, wnaṅ pariwaçaněn, haṅěměḥ haranya, hawani sakawtu, maṅka (23a) na waṅ wani
haṅrusak desaniṅ musuḥ, wadwaniṅ musuḥ, saholiḥnya, pinakalabha-
nya, mwa yan moliha māstakaniṅ musuḥ, saṅ prabhū, hataḍah adonan,
haṅalapi kaḷṅkāniṅ bhūmi, ndi ta ṅaran kaḷṅkāniṅ bhūmi, woṅ āṅūtil,
hambegal, hambahak, hambaranaṅ, maliṅ tuwi, hikā tā suṅana gañjaran,
phalanya hilaṅa rosanya, haṅatihati mapaṅeran, hikā ta çīlā wanī, tan
suṅanā haçriṅ haṅambaḥ nagarā riṅ jro purā, mewěḥ manahiṅ wanī,
waninya hamarikāla wadwa saṅ prabhū, hamaçeṣa wěwěṅkoniṅ tuwan,
hamrañani woṅ iṅ jro nagarā, sikāra waninya, hikā tanāna wani (23b)
ya maṅkana, yan āna çīlānya maṅkana, pariwaçaněn, tan damakna, ikā
taṅ āṣadya ṣadya dūdū, tan ājrih aprabhū, wnaṅ ḷburn, mewěḥ riṅ
buḍḍi wani, hapan tan lyan īkā magawe wěṛ, titigā kwehnya, mapa
lwirnya, çūrā, saraçwati, lākṣmī, mapa çūra, buḍḍi wani, mapa budi
saraçwatī, buddhi mariṅ kaguṇan, mwaṅ prajña, mapa lākṣmī, buḍḍi
kinahan iṅ çugiḥ, hikā ta liriṅ agawe wěṛ, hikā ta saṅ mahyun āsawita,
den eliṅ pamtuniṅ wěṛ // hana ratu putraniṅ sama ratu, wiçeṣa sira,
tan wěnaṅ haranāna prabhū, hyaṅhyaṅ ṅarānīrā, prabhū pwa sira,
haputra wiçeṣā, prabhū ṅāranirā, hana ratu tan wiçeṣa, haputra pwa
si (24a) ra, tan wěnaṅ haranā rājjāputra, dyaḥdyaḥ haranirā, hāputra
pwa sirā, hikā rājjāputra, mapan mtu sama rātu // o // iti nawanatya
kawruhakna // o // parisāmapta tlas inurat, riṅ bhūhtala mla // sukla-
pakṣa // dasamī // saptawara // ça // pañcawara // pa // warā //
dūkūt // thīthī // çaçih // kā // 3 // rah // 3 // těṅgěk // tuṅgal
// o //

RĀJAPATIGUNDALA

according to Ms. Or. Leyden 5056, p. 13a—18.

(*13a*) // o // awighnam āstu // o // oṃ adityaha namaḥ swāhā, oṃ
siddya triga dewaya nama swāhā, aprawiṣṭa, hana lkasnya, apagĕh kaṇ
rāt, amba taṇ bhūwana, sthiti mṛttha, çaddaçiwa jana wruha, padukā
çrī maharājaḥ dirajaḥ, çrī kṛtanagara triwikrama, mahārāja sama pwa
nugraha, sapolah saṇ prabhū, riṇ wka wet, kaṇ maṇḍala, hanak putu
buyut, haṅgas kṛpĕk, tan kawaraha deniṇ wakū haji hanaraji, sahala-
nira saṇ prabhū, āpan saṇ hyaṇ maṇḍala warggaji, brāhmā dewayajñā
hana raja maṇḍala, kunaṇ çarinira, hamaṅku saṇ hyaṅ rājapatiguṇḍala,
paṅĕrmban, paṅuluwuṇ, padagaṇ daluwaṇ, sakāpañjiṇ ṅiṇ kayaṅan,
para wulu, para taṇḍa sakapaṅguh, sakaṅuban denira saṇ hyaṇ maṇḍala,
salwiraniṇ ṅaçraha ri saṇ hyaṇ maṇḍala, kaṇ salampaḥ jnĕṅan deniṇ
wado bala saṇ nātha, tan kagiṅaṅa saṇ hyaṇ maṇḍala, liṇ **saṇ hyaṇ**
haji kṛtthanagarā, tan kawaraha deniṇ bhūmi rāt kabeh, saṇ hyaṇ
matala, tumus mariṇ wka wet saṇ hyaṇ maṇḍala, tan kalaṅalaṅan, tan
koluṅoluṅan // oṃ uma, brāhmā, wiṣṇu saṇ hyaṇ rājapatiguṇḍala
(*13b*), tan kawara deniṇ jagat, makaṅūni deniṇ bala saṇ prabhū, tan
kahirarakna rasa saṇ hyaṇ rājapatiguṇḍala, kapaṇguḥ denira saṇ
hyaṇ maṇḍala, lumraḥ riṇ sa yawadipa, çajñā haji, pamaripihira riṇ
jagat, hapan ana hiḍĕp arupaha yowaṇā, yan tanpa hiḍĕp, tan waluyahā,
kunaṇ saṇ prabhū, awak ṣadū, tumut swahawakā, hyaṇ mātuwa, ṛṣi,
brāhmāṇa, weçya, boḍḍa, manūḥ, raja, sarwwajanmā, makadi bahan
pūrwwa, kunaṇ saṇ wiku wnaṇ yogiçwaraha, saṇ siddapaṇḍita, sira
saṇ swargga hupti saṇ gambiçwara, tusniṇ wnaṇ dewaguruha // tan
ayu hanak ṣiçya, catū janmā ulukĕmbaṇ, kabayan, handadi dewaguru,
hana pwa caṇḍala kārmma, lumaku wikū, hadudukuḥ ta ikā, hana pwa
caṇḍala pāpa, hanapwana natar hikā, hana pwanak saṇ brāhmāṇa yan
iṇ sabraṇ, yan iṇ yawa, wwaṇbhaṇ, saṇ çewa hanaknya, çewaha, saṇ
boḍḍa hanaknya boḍḍaha, saṇ rāja hanaknya, rajaha, saṇ manūḥ
hanaknya, manūha, saṇ çūdra hanaknya sudraha, muwaḥ kaṇ sarwwa
janmā, hatutūra riṇ kāryyanira sowaṇ sowaṇ, hana pwa dewagurūha,
sira wnaṇ hagawe dewagurū, magaweha ṛṣi kabeh, wasi maṅuyu, haṅa-
jar, (*14a*), habābaru, hagawe hayu, hana pwa saṇ brāhmāṇa yan tan-

pañāskara riṇ brāhmāṇa, tan brāhmāṇa ikā, çewa yan pañāskaraha riṇ
çewa tan sewa hikā, boddạ yan tanpañāskaraha riṇ boddā, tan bodda
hikā // tanda ṅaranya, haywa tan bhakti haguru, marapwan tanpa
maṅgih hupadĕṇda, salwiraniṇ wikū, haywa hana winehan haṅera riṇ
tani, uniweḥ yan hana mimikunana, rampas taṇ den wiçiçi, patyani, saṇ
walaka, misikana, patyani, çatrū saṇ prabhū ikā, ka, tan kṛttā kaṇ
bhūwaṇa hikā denya, pañawak iṅ mahapralaya ṅaranya hikā, hana
pañĕrmban, guru panti, hakris guru panti, hakris guru pajaran, haṅa-
ṅgoha bhawaniṇ āwikwawikwan, haywa wineh tumawaça, yan duruṇ
pañāskara riṇ saṇ yogiçwarā, hamañca karmma, haṅlukis, haywa bina-
san ĕmpu, haṅlĕtuhi çewa hikā, kunaṇ pañca patapan, ṅaranya, pṛthiwi,
hapah, teja, bāyu, hakaça, saṅ atapa riṇ pṛthiwi, banwa luka, saṇ atapa
ṅupah, amĕṇ ṅamĕṇ, saṅ atapeṇ tejā, saṇ yogiçwarā dewaguru, saṅ
atapeṇ bāyū, tetegā, saṅ atapeṇ hakaça, saṅ maṅajar, sama eliṅa (14b)
riṇ çaçaṇanira sowaṇ sowaṇ, sira saṇ yogiçwara, sira wnaṇ adum apiliḥ,
wnaṇ hakalambiha guru hapayuṅā, asaṅgaha, çiwapataraṇa kamaṇda-
lu, hagĕṇtagĕṇtā, makarawiṣtā, ka wnaṇ sira maṅāskarani, sabhāwa
lākṣaṇanira, kunaṇ ṛṣi, tan pidda dewaguruha, kaṇ tan dewagurūha //
saṇ kṛno cedaṅgā, salwiraniṇ kataman daçamala, tan wnaṇ dewagurūha,
yan hana maṇkāna, sapihana, yan arp dewagurūha, hakūmĕl kaṇ rāt
denya // utpatha çrī saṇ nātha, salahaknā riṇ raçikanya, kahawaknya pwa
ya, alkasa biça çayanaha, maraheṇ saṇ yogiçwara, hanuta raṣaniṇ dewa giri
lālawu, hampĕkana dahana karuwat pāpaniṇ bhūwanā, kunaṇ yan hana
maṅkānā, ilaṇ kaṇ pawitraniṇ bhuwanā denya, yan tan kulawiçūdda, kunaṇ
ya gawe dewaguruhā, haywa tumandaṇ, hakalambi guru, haṅera daga-
niṇ guru, diwaçanya, pituṇ ṅlek pituṇ wṅi, han widi de saṇ yogiçwarā.
hagaweya dewaguru, hulukĕmbaṇ, kabayan, dewaguru yañ catūr janmā, hana pwa wikū histri, haṅarpākna pakilyan, aṅhiṇ sasadu, haywa
sinidigawe, bwat altu (15a) ḥ saṇ prabhū, makaṅūni kaṇ bhūwaṇa,
makawana, kweḥ maraṇnā, yan tan dṛwiṇ kaliṅan sasadū // kunaṇ tri
kayañan, wuddi wariṅin, hambulu cacaruniṇ bañjaran, salwiraniṇ sarwwa
tinandur, sĕñjaṇ pañcuran, simpurūṇ, patani, gilaṇ-gilaṇ, pahyasan, yatha
yaça ṅaranya, asūṇ mās pirāk, riṇ saṇ wikū, yatha yaça ṅaranya, tan
dewayajñā, āmbhuthayajñā, abrāhmāyajñā ya, toyayajñā ya, kunaṇ saṇ
yogiçwarā, atirtthaniṇ jagat, tapanira hayaça, āna darmma çūnya, āna
darmma çastra, ikā ta darmma saṇ wikū, mataṅhyan saṇ yogiçwara, haywa
hinawara deniṇ jagat, āpan sira tirtthaniṇ bhūwanā, mnĕṇ kaṇ prama-
naniṇ rāt, kāryyanira ṅukuṣakĕn dupā, riṇ çūklapakṣa, makaṅūni hana-
dah akinkin darmma, bumi lwirnya, jumput kuluwut, kaṇlaṇ, kalaṅ-
gyān, kaputrawaṅçān, tani, hanālaga dalun, salwiraniṇ bhūmi carik,

lmah aheŋ, tan salah amūktyakna, gunūŋ, pasir, patarā tanya, bhūmi-
nira saŋ yogiçwara, tan salah amūktihā, saṅ atapa jugā mūktyakna,
tan purihĕn deniŋ jagat, āpan ulihira hatoḥ pati, tan kawaraha deniŋ
(15b) çarāt, deniŋ manūh, āpan ulihira hatoḥ pati, tan kawarahana
deniŋ çarāt, deniŋ manūh, āpan ulihira hatoḥ pati juwita, maripakṣa
po sira saŋ maṅawara, yaça kacarintika riŋ āganal alit, saŋ maṅawara
karṣyan, kabrāhmānan, kasewakan, kaboḍḍan, ikā ta ḍarmma ḷwiḥ, tan
salah amūktyakna, paŋūluwūŋ, yan tan anā muṅguh tan salah caṇḍaka,
saŋ nātha çrī mahārajā dirajā, sirā hamitkatana rāt, yan tan hana hiḍĕp,
oṃ namu namu wastu // karṣyan sa yogiçwarā hamūktiha kabrāhmāna
hamūktiha kaçewan, saŋ çewa hamūktiha kaçewan, saŋ boḍḍa hamūktiha kaboḍḍan, tan salah caṇḍaka, tan salah hamūktiha, paṅuluwūŋ,
eliṅa kaṇṭanira sowaŋ sowaŋ, tan kawaraha deniŋ sarāt, ana ḍarmma,
noreŋ tapakan, tan darmma ṅaran, hananiŋ sarwwa janmā kabeh,
haywa tan eliŋ ṅiŋ pitkĕtira rajapatiguṇḍala, yan hana harp arupa
yowanaha, haywa tan eliŋ ṅiŋ bhūktinira sowaŋ sowaŋ, sama heliṅa
riŋ kĕṇḍĕŋ, sĕṅkĕrira sowaŋ sowaŋ, kunaŋ yan hana hamicarani (16a)
yan apatut lawan agara, wnaŋ huwahana, hana tha ya ka hakonkon
digu, yeka ṅawas kaŋ den kon, patyanira pa saŋ makonkon, aŋhṛmĕk
saŋ hyaŋ kamaṇḍalu, aŋhṛmĕk pakuṇḍan, ṅa, / kṛmi sampeka durat-
maka, saŋ prabhū ikā, kunaŋ ka yan amūjā, saŋ yogiçwara, tan hana
niŋ ṅamidihakĕn, çūḍḍa ça tinaṅapira taku, haywa tan aṅilaṅakĕn
raṣa saŋ hyaŋ rajapatiguṇḍala, yan arp arupa yowarṇnaha. yan amūjā
saŋ yogiçwarā, saŋ manūh hanampaha tirttha riŋ kuṇḍi maṇik, kṛttha
paraniŋ pūjā saŋ hyaŋ kamaṇḍalū, lūmbraḥ riŋ bhūmi sayawadipā,
makadi laṅĕṅanira saŋ prabhū siniwi riŋ sayawadipā, haga maṇik tan
kawaraha, pamūktinira riŋ jagat, saŋ prabhū rumākṣaha riŋ patapanira
saŋ yogiçwarā, tapanira saŋ ṛṣi, tapanira saŋ brāhmāna, saŋ çogattha,
saŋ çewa, saŋ boḍḍa, saŋ wado bala saŋ prabhū, ṅuniyuni saŋ manūh
rumākṣaha, saŋ yogiçwara, çaçalaḥ paḍa sila ṅaranya, kunaŋ yan amūjā
saŋ ṛṣi, sandura sakiŋ tani sahagaṅan, pahoman paduluraniŋ manūh,
yan amūjā saŋ yogiçwarā, (16b) saŋ manūh tanpa middiha, sakasu-
kaira taṅapĕn, āpan dṛwe yaṣa, dṛwyāhanira saŋ yogiçwara, maṅusi-
tĕhaniŋ çarira, dṛwyanira saŋ yogiçwara ikā, yan sira hayaça, mataṅyan
haywa pinarikṣa, apan sira wiṣya mṛttha, dṛwyanira saŋ yogiçwarā,
hana kāryyanira saŋ yogiçwarā, saŋ manūḥ warahĕn ujar kelā, maŋ-
kāna yan hana maṅāskarā, tan kna riŋ harik puriḥ, saha prakara, āpan
sira ṅukusakĕn dupa, kṛtthaha niŋ jagat, laṅĕṅanira saŋ prabhū,
siniwi riŋ sayawadipā, karyyanira siniwi wikū hamūjā, handohakna
maraṇa, kāryyanirā, kunaŋ yan hana ḍarmma ṅĕlūd, yan hana dṛpaniṅ

atuṅgu ḍarmma, saṇ prabhū hañiliṅakna, yan tan lumaṅlaṅ irikā, saṇ
prabhū patakā, yan tan lumaṅlan i ḍarmma, hana ta ḍarmma sinaṅguḥ
sagata, yan sāmpun, lpas iṇ pañāskara, kṛttha saya muwaḥ, hana
maṅrundaḥ patakā, kunaṇ dupan saṅāskarā ḍarmma, marapwan
tumut çwargganiṅ āḍarmma, piṅewu ta janmā, riṇ ṅadana çwargga,
tumus mariṇ wka wet putu buyut hituṇ, haṅgas kṛpĕk, mataṅhyan ta
saṇ sūja (17a) nmāha, haywak tan eliṇ riṇ pamĕkasira saṇ hyaṇ
rajāpatiguṇḍala // kunaṇ dṛwya muleha riṇ gusti, gusti muleha riṇ
taṇḍa, taṇḍa muleha riṇ mantri, mantri muleha riṇ ratu, ratu muleha
riṇ wikū, wikū muleha riṇ dewa, dewa muleha riṇ hyaṇ, hyaṇ muleha
riṇ çūnya, sarūpahan, ya ta kopadarwwaha, wastu matmahana hĕṇḍĕp-
ĕṇḍĕp, oṃ namū namū wastu, oṃ catūr açrama tan yowanā janmānya,
papagakĕna riṇ bhaṭāra kala, tutĕn pĕraṅĕn, dmakn iṇ macan, kata-
ḍaha deniṇ detya danāwwa, kasambĕt deniṇ dṅĕn, katadaha deniṇ
bhūṭa, kapaluha deniṇ pĕpĕcatira hyaṇ komara, kabubata riṇ hikuḥnira
saṇ hyaṇ nāgha, babadĕn iṇ kbo, siniṅat niṇ sapi, tujahn iṇ gajah,
surudĕn iṇ warāk, sawutĕn deniṇ ṅula maṇḍi, tibāha hamamanek,
kasāmbĕrn iṇ glap tanpa hudan, katĕwĕka riṇ ṅamūk, urip tan warasā,
wuduga, saṅāra, edana, buyana, hutāha, siṅkĕla, yata sakwehiṇ tan
paṅidĕpakĕn, kahupatanana denira saṇ hyaṇ rājapatiguṇḍalā, tumamaha
mariṇ tan pahidĕppa (17b) kĕn, oṃ wastu sarwwa wighnā lara roghga,
kabuktiha deniṇ tan paṅidĕpakĕn, tan kĕna tambanana, sadakalā pata-
kahā, maṇkānā hupatanira çri bhagati, saṇ sa ratu riṇ ṅalawas.
lumraḥ riṇ sayawadipā, wāstu tumaha mariṇ wetbet, kaṇ hutpata, yapwan
si hahiḍĕp, urip warasa ratuha wikuha, catūr janmāha, raksanĕn deniṇ
hyaṇ, hyaṇ triyoḍḍaçakṣi, samaṇkāna rasa saṇ hyaṇ rajapatiguṇḍala,
pitkĕtira çrī bhāti, saṇ ratu riṇ ṅalawas, āpan samahiriṇ saṇ paṇḍata,
mataṅhyan ta saṇ sujanmā, haywa tan eliṇ iṇ kĕṇḍĕṇ sĕṇkĕrira, marapwan rupa yowaṇnā, oṃ we yapwan rūpa yowaṇna, oṃ weya nāma-
swahā // o // iti saṇ hyaṇ rajapatiguṇḍalā, cinandi lawan dewaçaçaṇā,
paṇgawayni saṇ ratu riṇ ṅalawas // o // oṃ çorabhyoḥ, ajite ḍarmma,
oṃ A A A, oṃ oṃ I Bra I, oṃ U I Ndri U, oṃ E Jha E, oṃ Ma Ma
Ma, oṃ sarwwapāpaharayaḥ, oṃ Çri wastu // oṃ garḍḍipatayaya
swaha, tan kaparaga riṇ phaladĕṇḍa, oṃ astu, oṃ labdawara cittamani,
oṃ sadya (18a) stu te namaha swaha // o // iti saṇ hyaṇ rajapatiguṇḍala, cinandi lawan dewaçaçaṇā, paṇgawayni saṇ ratu riṇ ṅalawas,
çrī bhathati, āpasĕṅgahan çrī kṛtthanagara, pinakabalūṇbhaṇ ṅi saṇ
yogiçwarā, pinakṛttharahayūnira saṇ paṇḍita, apitūtūr i rājanagara,
sawado bala saṇ prabhū // o //.

PURWADIGAMA, PREAMBLE,

according to Dr H. N. van der Tuuk's

Kawi-Balineesch—Nederlandsch Woordenboek,

sub voce *ḍarmmāḍyakṣa.*

———

nihan pratyeka sang bhujangga çiwān minakasthawira ring nagara,
sang kumĕmit mamangku sanghyang ādigamaçāstrasārodrĕta, lwirnira,
sang pinakaprabhrĕti, sang āryya dharmmādhyakṣa lyan sangkerika,
wwalu kwehnya, ndya ta, sang āryya tirwan, sang āryya kaṇḍamuhi,
sang āryya pamwatan, sang āryya panjyajiwa, sang āryya manghuri,
sang āryya jambi, sang āryya lekan, sang āryya tangar, ndah samang-
kana lwirning linggihnira, kapwa bhujangga haji sira kabeh.

———

PRANITI RAJA KAPA-KAPA,

according to Ms. Or. Leyden 1850.

——

Metre: Ḍaṇḍaṅ-gula, *stanzas of 10 verses each:*

verse	1 : 10	*syllables, vowel of last syllable:*					*i*
,,	2 : 10	,,	,,	,, ,,	,,	:	*a*
,,	3 : 8	,,	,,	,, ,,	,,	:	*e or o*
,,	4 : 7	,,	,,	,, ,,	,,	:	*u*
,,	5 : 9	,,	,,	,, ,,	,,	:	*i*
,,	6 : 7	,,	,,	,, ,,	,,	:	*a*
,,	7 : 6	,,	,,	,, ,,	,,	:	*u*
,,	8 : 8	,,	,,	·, ,,	,,	:	*a*
,,	9 : 12	,,	,,	,, ,,	,,	:	*i*
,,	10 : 7	,,	,,	,, ,,	,,	:	*a*

Stanza 1: nihan namarna reh pranitinniṅ
raja kapa kapa pinnardika
mariñci basa mantrinne
tĕgĕsse ma pan luhuṅ
tri titiga sĕtya kaṅ ḍiṅin
sadu kapiṅ kaliḥnya
kapiṅ tiga tuhu
wṛdiniṅ sĕtya winarna
milweṅ lara duka wiraṇnya hiṅ gusti
lwirriṅ sadu hiñucap //

Stanza 2: hajriḥ yen naṅriyinnana kapti
nora mĕḍar kĕkĕrraniṅ ṇatha
lwir riṇkaṅ tuhu karppe
tansaḥ caḍaṅ ñiṅ kayun
nora giṇsir hiṅ saṅgup nĕṅgih
tan rumasa yen gaḍaḥ

hiŋ paŋwasannipun
hiya hiku hiŋkaŋ ńaran
basa mantri tuwin ta hińucap maliḥ
mantri moñcanagara //

Stanza 3 : tumĕŋguŋ dĕmaŋ lan roŋga nĕŋgiḥ
kaṇḍuruwan lan patiḥ punnika
denin ta patiḥ wṛdine
kaŋ nampurnakkĕn niku
parentaḥhe çri ṇaraphathi
tompa sacipteŋ ṇatha
denne ta tumĕŋguŋ
hiŋkaŋ ŋahulaḥ gagaman
lan ńawruḥhi koŋkonnanniŋ ṇaraphathi
denin wṛdinniŋ dĕmaŋ //

Stanza 4 : kaŋ ńahulaḥ paŋńaŋge sakyeḥniŋ
raja kaputren lan paŋńaŋgennya
kaŋ para mantri sakeḥhe
kaŋ kasarireŋ phrabhu
lwirriŋ roŋga kaŋ ńulaḥ nĕŋgiḥ
sisikon padaḷmman
nira çań aphrabhu
myaŋ rakittiŋ pasaŋgraḥhan
kaṇḍuruwan kaŋ ńannampunnakkĕn nĕŋgiḥ
parentaḥhiŋ papatya //

Stanza 5 : yata jĕnĕńiŋkaŋ para mantri
bujoŋga harya mańuri lawan
harya leka lan maliye
harya jamba punniku
harya tiron harya papati
harya tiron punnika
binubuḥhan saguŋ
ńiŋ pakarya denne harya
hamańuri bubuḥhanne hanampunni
mantri bujoŋga samya //

Stanza 6 : tĕgĕssiŋkaŋ mańuri winarni
wani mati kalawan prayoga
aṇḍamohi hiŋ tĕgĕsse

pañjaŋ jiwa punniku
pandĕḷggan kaŋ ṅulaḥ nĕŋgiḥ
tĕnuŋ gĕgĕriŋ ṅika
jomba leka nĕŋguḥ
lwirña hamot hulaḥ hulam
lawan maliḥ punnika waṅĕnniŋ mantri
bujoŋgarya tironnya //

Stanza 7: haŋrapĕtkĕn kaŋ ṅarṅgaŋ nĕŋgiḥ
lan hañjaganni laganniŋ mĕŋsaḥ
mantri pasĕppanniŋ praje
harja wirasiṅeku
harya wiraraja lan maliḥ
harya siṅasarika
deniŋ tĕgĕssipun
pasĕppan punniku apan
laŋlaŋ dalu kaŋ ṅasor sakiŋ punniki
nĕŋgiḥ harya pamottan //

Stanza 8: palimpiŋṅan pakulutan maliḥ
surantanni pan bubuḥhannira
haŋḷpaskĕn kaguŋṅanne
lan haṅrkṣa kaḍatun
deniŋ jĕnĕṅiŋ çeṇaphathi
siṅa kaŋ nuduḥhĕna
hiŋ parentaḥ hiku
wĕnaŋ ṅaran seṇaphatya
deniŋ mantri paṅalasan niku nĕŋgiḥ
pura haŋraramunya //

Stanza 9: kyeḥhiŋ mantri satus sekĕt nĕŋgiḥ
kaliḥ bĕlaḥ sewu patya taṇḍa
wadyaji haṅabehine
taṇḍa lan maliḥhipun
ya phañji handaka lan maliḥ
kajinĕmman dene ta
maliḥ hiŋsorripun
hadiphathi kuwu lawan
saŋ ṅanden bubuyut paṅalassan nĕṅgiḥ
panakatenniŋ ṇatha //

Stanza 10 : samya hulaḥ kaŋ sineren něŋgiḥ
sakaṭaḥhe woŋ kriḍa punnika
titi tammat pranitine
raja kapa-kapeku
mugestuwa pañakṣamanniŋ
tunna laŋkuŋñiŋ basa
binastuweŋ kayun
nira çaŋ maha pamaṣa
santosarja sarajya lir tarumakiŋ
sěḍěŋ muwaḥ kawarsan //

AN ECCLESIASTICAL GENTLEMAN, V. PAGE V.

CHARTERS
TEXTS

SARWADHARMA CHARTER
1269 A.D.
according to Brandes-Krom, *Oud-Javaansche Oorkonden,*

vol. II, 1913, p. 188.

Plate 1, verso,
line 1: swasti çrī çakawarṣātīta, i çaka 1191, karttikamāsa tithi pañcami çū

2: klapakṣa, wā, ka, wṛ, wāra langkir, uttarāsāḍhā nakṣatra, wiçwade

3: wata, gaṇḍa yoga, wairājya muhūrtta, baruṇaparwweça, walawa karaṇa,

4: mṛcchīka rāçi, irika diwaçanyājñā çrī sakalajagatnatheça, nārasinghamūrttyani

5: nditaparākrama, açeṣarājānyacuḍāmaṇinārpitabharaṇārawinda, çokasantapi

6: tasujanahṛdayāmbujāwawodhanaswabhāwa çrī kṛtanagaranāmabhiṣeka, tinaḍaḥ de rakrya

7: n mahāmantri katriṇi rakryan mantri hino, rakryan mantri sirikan, rakryan mantri halu, umingsor i para taṇḍa

Plate 2, recto,
line 1: rakryan ri pakirakiran makabehan rakryan apatiḥ makasikasir kbo arĕma, rakryan dmung

2: mapañji wipakṣa, rakryan kanuruhan mapañjyanurida, makadi sang mantri wāgmima

3: ya, paranitijña, nūṣāntaramadhuranāthānukulakāraṇa, mapasĕnggahan sang rāma

4: pati, tan kawuntat sang pamgat i tirwan ḍang ācāryya dharmmadewa, sang pāmgĕt ing kaṇḍamuhi

5: ḍang ācāryya smaradahana, sang pamgĕt i manghuri ḍang ācāryya smaradewa, sang pamgĕt ing jamba ḍang ā

6 : cāryya çiwanātha, sang pamgĕt ing pañjang jīwa ḍang ācāryya
graja, mpungku dharmmadhyakṣa ri kaçe

7 : wan ḍang ācāryya çiwanātha, mapañji tanutama, i pingsorny-
ajñā çrī mahārāja ku

Plate 2, verso,

line 1: monakĕn   ring kabuyutan ri lokeçwara, tkeng
wiṣaya punpunan sang hyang

2 : sarwwadharmma, parhyangan,   ityewamādi,
padamla

3 : kna sang hyang rājapraçāsti macihna kṛtanagara kapang-
kwan i wiṣaya punpunan   sang hyang sa

4 : rwwadharmma magĕhakna pangrakṣa çrī mahārāja ri kaswatantran sang hyang sarwwadharmma, sambandha mpu

5 : ngku dharmmadhyakṣa mapañji tanutama, dinulur deni wiṣaya
punpunan sang hyang sarwwadharmma

6 :   ing bhūmi janggala pangjalu, pinakasopana-
nyan

7 : kĕn

sowang

Plate 3, recto,

line 1: sowang *byĕt* hajyan lakwalakwan adoh aparĕ, amijilakĕn pada*d*ar, pa*md*iha*n*, paga   .

2 : rĕm, mareng juru, buyut, kabayan, aweḥ patumbak tamwi,
panghulu bañu   ngūnɩ

3 : ngūni pamūjākĕn tahun, paḍacangan, yatikānmahakĕn trāsa-
nya, an tinitiḥ bcik

4 : dening thāni bala, pinisakitan tan kinawruhinanya, nimittanyan apulung rahyangi

5 : nḍid bhṛta sakawat bhūming janggala pangjalu, marĕk ri
sang rāmapati, mwang ri rakryan apatiḥ makaso

6 : pana mpungku dharmmadhyakṣa mapañji tanutama, sang
rāmapati, pwa sakatadharmmacintana, tan *hup* tan

7 : kuminkin ing karakṣāning sarwwadharmma, pitowi pwan hana
turunyānugraha bhaṭāra jaya çrī wiṣṇuwa

Plate 3, verso,

line 1: rddhana irikang sarwwadharmman sapiha sakeng thāni bala,
ngūnīkāla sang apañji patipati dha

2 : rmmādhikāraṇa, nimittanyan enak ka kaniçcayan iki pininto-
nakĕn sang apañji tanuta

3: ma ri sang rāmapati, karaṇa sang rāmapati dinulur de rakryan apatiḥ sacchāya mwang sang apañji ta
4: nutama, marĕk ri çrī mahārāja ring wiṣaya punpunan sang
hyang sarwwadharmma, mratisubaddhakna panapih bha
5: ṭāra jaya çrī wiṣṇuwarddhana, ring wiṣaya punpunan sang
hyang sarwwadharmma sakeng thāni bala, makadona
6: kaswatantran sang hyang sarwwadharmma, mangdadyakna
sthīratarani palinggiḥ çrī mahārāja ring ratnasingha
7: sana, pinakekacātraning sayawadwipa, pinakottunggadewa
sang samantaprabhu ring bhūmi

Plate 4, recto,
line 1: janggala pangjalu, mangkana rasani hatur sang rāmapati,
winuriwuri deni hatur akryan apati
2: ḥ pinirĕsĕpakĕn deni sang apañji tanutama, çrī mahārāja
prabhu dewangça, dharmmamū
3: rttyawatāra, inahakĕn bhaṭāra paramakāraṇa, sumapwana ka-
lĕngkaning bhūwana, munarjīwakna
4: sarwwadharmma, malwyaknang jagaddhita, makawyakti gati
sang prabhu, an satyādiwihitaçīlānucāra,
5: pitowi pwan kakawaça deni hatur ning paḍa wāgmimaya,
sarisaryy anghaturakĕn heyopade
6: ya, kāraṇa çrī mahārāja, an wawang manganumoda ri hatur
sang rāmapati, dinulur
7: de rakryan apatiḥ sacchāya mwang sang apañji tanutama, an
tikang wiṣaya punpunan sang hyang sa

Plate 4, verso,
line 1: rwwadharmma, sapiha sakeng thāni bala, maryy anūtakna
byĕt ḍanghani thāni bala, byĕt hajya
2: n agöng aḍmit, lakwalakwan adoh aparö, turunturun sagĕm
sarakut sakeng thāni
3: bala, maryy amijilakna padadar, pamḍihan, pagagarĕm, mareng juru, buyut, kabaya
4: n, maryy aweha papiṇḍa pa[ng]ti, patiklanggas, panghulu
bañu, mareng thāni balanya, sowang so
5: wang, kunĕng yan panuku bañu ikang thāni bala pangaçra-
yanya, tumatātukwa sapanut sa
6: ni sawaḥnya ikang kalagyan, tanpa mijilakna panulis, kunĕng
ikang tan pgat awijila

7: knanya mareng thāni bala, pamūjā juga, wyaktyanyan tan
pgata pamaraçrayanya ring thani bala

Plate 5, recto,

line 1: yapwan hana kaharĕp sang prabhu rikang wiṣaya punpunan
sang hyang sarwwadharmma, byĕt hajyanan, lakwa

2: lakwan, pintapalaku salwiranya kewala katĕmwa ri mpungku
dharmmadhyakṣa juga, tan kahawa

3: ta sakeng thāni bala, kunĕng kolahulaha sang hyang rājapraçāsti an pinūjā denikang wiṣa

4: ya punpunan sang hyang sarwwadharmma, amagut apajöng
kuning, acuringa rahina wngi, ndan haywa tekang wiṣa

5: ya punpunan sang hyang sarwwadharmmānghiras watĕk,
angiwwa rare, abañwabañwa, apugata, awarawaranga ri

6: khalani kapūjān sang hyang rājapraçāsti, muwah kawnangakn
ikang wiṣaya punpunan sang hyang sarwwadharmma kha

7: lang kalagyan, paryyangan, mwang dharmma jumput, ri kā-
lanyan pamūjā ri sang hyang prasāda kabhaktyan

Plate 5, verso,

line 1: sowang sowang, wnang ajnwahalang, asumping tuñjung sini-
wak, muwah anugraha çrī mahārāja

2: amaluyakĕn kaswatantran sang hyang sarwwadharmma, tan
kaknana de sang wiṣaya punpunan sang hyang sarwwa

3: dharmma ri pamḍang tanghiran, pakudur panghurang, pakris,
pasraḥ anganggwawalī, tuwuḥ watu, huri

4: p anak, kĕmbang i pöng tutuñjung, tĕpĕl sang ratu tunggak
ning garyyang, nawagraha, nagapuspa, wnang a

5: nusuna salö, aguntinge ruhur bale, wnang añjamaha kawula,
amupuha kawulenakwakĕ

6: n, amupuha ngrahana, ingirup ingirir ing parud amangana sal-
wirning rājamangça kadya

7: ngganing baḍawang, wḍus gunting, karung puliḥ, pjahaning
rara, asu tugĕl, ananĕma kamale rumambat i

Plate 6, recto,

line 1: ngumah, ananĕma kĕmbang kunĕ ri harĕpan, ananĕma galu-
guḥ, adṛwya patĕtĕngahan aja

2: ngw agaḍing, ikang juru kula, mangkana rasanyanugraha çrī
kṛtanagara ri wiṣaya punpunan sa

3: rwwadharmma sakawat bhūmi janggala pangjalu, ri wruhani-
kang sakala jana ryyatiçayani kadharmmaparā

4 : yanan çrī mahārāja an pinakekacchātraning sayawadwīpa, maluyakĕn pangekī

5 : kṛtābhūmi janggala pangjalu, matangyan dadi ta sang hyang rājapraçāsti, malawölawö kṛtanaga

6 : ra, magĕhakĕn kaswatantran sang hyang sarwwadharmma, sampun umunggwing ripta, hinlĕpan pitawastra, pinangkwa

7 : kĕn irikang wiṣaya dharmma samudāya, ri sanmata para taṇḍa rākryan makabehan, manghaturakn i

Plate 6, verso,

line 1 : kang wiṣaya dharmma, sā( )na, kā, 1, sū, 3, ri çrī mahārāja pamuspanyan sampun kṛtānu

2 : graha, kunĕng ri sḍĕnganya hana ngruddhāmungkilmungkila ri rasa sang hyang rājapraçāsti, salwiranya

3 : yadyan caturwarṇna, brahmaṇa, kṣatriya, weçya, çudra, athawa, caturaçrama, brahmācāri,

4 : gṛhastha, wanaprastha, bhikṣuka, makādi sang prabhu mantry anagata, mwang pinghay ākurug anak thāni ya

5 : wat umulahulah i rasa sang hyang rājapraçāsti, tan atguḥ karakṣan i kaswatantran sang hyang sarwwadharmma

6 : tasmat kabyĕt karmmaknanya, sakulagotranyāmuktya phalaning pātaka mahāpātaka, atipāta

7 : ka, phalanyan manghulahakĕn hanyayaprawṛtti, kawulakan de sang hyang trayodaça sākṣī, ā

Plate 7, recto,

line 1 : ditya candrā pānilonalaçcā, dyoḥ bhūmirāpohṛdayaṃ yamāçca, āhaçca rātra

2 : çca tathāçcasanmyā dharmmaçca jānākinarāyawṛttaṃ, mangkana pwa, yo rājānugraham hatwā,

3 : mohat murkho naro hi saḥ, parāparakulais sarwwaiḥ, rorawaṃ yantu sarwwadā, yawat bhū

4 : tanikaḥ sṛṣṭwā, tāwad janmi punar yyadi, kṣudra jantu çariraṇi, prāpnuyarcca narodhama, ya

5 : di syān mānuṣibhūtaḥ, kliwaḥ kuṣṭaçca bāmaṇaḥ, an ( ) omattohyapasmaro, kubjaḥ pa

6 : ngguh kunis tathā, nahan katmahanyan dadi wwang ri huwusnyan tumĕmpuḥ ring mahārorawa //ā

7 : stu astu astu// oṃ nama çiwāya // o //

104

DECREE JAYA SONG,

about 1350 A.D.

according to Brandes-Krom, *Oud-Javaansche Oorkonden*,
vol. II, 1913, p. 207.

Incomplete.

Plate 2, recto,
line 1: çeka dyah hayām wuruk, iniring denyājñā pāduka çrī tribhuwanottungga rājadewī jaya wisnuwa
   2: rddhanī sakalarājamanggalabhawatīpratima, lalitamanohara-
jñānapratāpaçobhita, sārddhanāri
   3: çwara muang pāduka bhaṭāra çrī kṛtawarddhana, açeṣarāja-
praṇipatamāṇḍitā, sacchaya muang ājña pā-
   4: duka çrī wijayadewī, mahārājarājaçekarādhiṣṭitāninditawīryy-
alangkarā, sakalaguṇapra-
   5: wālabuddhisahitā, sārddhanārīçwara muang pāduka bhaṭāra
çrī wijayarājasā, sanggramawīryyalangkṛta

Plate 2, verso,
line 1: tinaḍah de rakryan mahāmantrī katrīṇi rakryan mahāmantrī
i hino, dyah īçwara, rakryan mahāmantrī
   2: sirikan,dyah ipo, rakryan mantri i halu dyah kañcing, umingsor i taṇḍa rakryan ring pakirakiran ma
   3: kabehan, sang āryya senapati pu tanu, sang āryyātmarāja pu
taṇḍing, rakryan dmung pu gaṣṭi, rakryan ka
   4: nuruhan pu turut, rakryan rangga pu lurukan, rakryan tuměnggung pu nāla, sādugopika durjjanawi
   5: nigrahatatpara, mawastha patih ri pajang, samahiring muang
rake juru pangalasan pu pṭul nayawi

Plate 3, recto,
line 1: nayadhara, makapramuka samantrīnggitājñā prajālangkarā, rake mapatih pu mada, sakalanītiwṛha
2: spatisanggrāmikā, prāṇarakṣaka çrī mahārāja pranalāmratisubaddhakĕn pangḍiri çrī mahārājā
3: ngkĕn içwarapratiwimba, gumawayakĕn hitakarmmaning yawadwipamāṇḍala, muang wiçirṇnaning prangmu
4: ke pāduka çrī mahārāja, dharmmadhyakṣa ring kaçewan, sang āryya rājaparākrama, ḍang ācā
5: ryya dharmmarāja, dharmmadhyakṣa ring kasogatan, sang āryyadhirāja ḍang ācāryya kanakamuni,

Plate 3, verso,
line 1: boddhaçāstrawyākaraṇaparisamāpta, tlas karuhun sang dharmmaprawakta wyawahārawicchedaka, sang pamgĕ
2: t i tiruan, sang āryya wangçādhirāja, ḍang ācāryya çiwanātha, bhairawapakṣa nyayawyakaraṇaça
3: straparisamāpta, samgĕt i kaṇḍamuhi, ḍang ācāryya marmmanātha, mapañjy āngçuman, sorapakṣa nyāyawya
4: karaṇaçāstraparisamāpta, samgĕt i manghuri, ḍang ācāryya smaranātha, bhairawapakṣa nyāyawyaka
5: raṇaçāstraparisamāpta, samgĕt i jāmba, ḍang ācāryya jayasmara, sorapakṣa çangkyaçāstraparisamā

Plate 4, recto,
line 1: pta, samgĕt i pamuatan ḍang ācāryyāgreçwara bhairawapakṣa nyāyawyakaraṇaçastraparisamāpta
2: samgĕt i kaṇḍangan rarai, ḍang ācāryya munīndra boddhaçāstraparisamāpta, mangrasarasani sangka ri göngniya
3: dimuktinikang wyawahāri kālih, kumwa pgat kawiwakṣanya de sang pragwiwāka matguh ri kapakṣadharmman
4: ri dalĕm nāgara, marmmanikang wyawahari kālih sacchaya mampakāmpak humatur i taṇḍa rakryan ring
5: pakirakiran makabehan mintonakĕn pakṣanya sowang-sowang kunĕng sungan warawarah aki

Plate 4, verso,
line 1: santana, mapañji çaraṇa, muang sarowangnya, ki karṇna, mapañji manākara, ajaran reka, ki siran, ki jumput
2: ungsun madṛwya lmah punang manah i manuk, kayoning sawah, aḍawung, lirih l, i berĕm, lirih l, i pa

3: jnon kiduling umah, lirih 2, pajnon kubwan, kuñci 1, pange-
ran, kubwan, kuñci 1, tiga thani, ka

4: yoning sawah wareng, lirih 1, kayon waluntas, lirih 10, tiga
thani kubwan, kuñci 1, dinanā

5: kĕn ing tuhatuha maring katyagan pakaṇḍangan, lirih 16,
maring maṇḍala ring kuku, lirih 2, maring jangganing pa

Plate 5, recto,
line 1: ngle, lirih 1, kabhukti dening amadṛwyakĕn lirih 33, piṇḍah
lirih 67, punika ta sthiti bhukti sangkeng tu

2: hatuha, bapa, kaki buyut, pitung, anggas, muning, kṛpĕk, tan
hanang suwanda, apan anadi kabhuktyanipun, maka

3: wyakti kirttini tuhatuhani ungsun bale i maṇḍala i kasḍahan,
sakakala 919, wayuhanĕngah ra

4: kwa aranipun, punika ta samanakāla lāwan sawah, apituwin
tan hana sawahipun samasānak i punang sī

5: ma tiga, liwat ing watĕs pakaṇḍangan, tan punika ḍawakta
lmah i ungsun tanpatahil tan kajnĕngan ta

Plate 5, verso,
line 1: n pinakaparanati dening deça, makahetu anadi kābhuktyani-
pun, tan wruh ta ungsun panangkanipun a

2: pan anadi, mangke ta inakunipun pasaṇḍan pun samasānak i
sīma tiga, makādi pun apañjyanawung harṣa, kunĕng

3: sungan warawarah samasānak i sīma tiga, makādi sang apanjy
anawung harṣa, ungsun madṛwya punang lmah sawidah

4: pitung lirih wicarawisaya, sinaṇḍakĕn i pitung i ungsun ing
pirak kalitngah takĕr, duk punang bhumi jawa tanpa ga

5: gaman pisis ika tang pakṣa kālih, pinametakĕn çastradṛṣṭa,
deçadṛṣṭa, udāharaṇa, guru kaka,

Plate 6, recto,
line 1: makatanggwan rasāgama ri sang hyang kuṭāramānawādi,
manganukāra prawṛttyacāra sang pāṇḍita wyawahārawiccheda

2: ka ring puhun malama, atĕhĕr taṇḍa rakryan motus atañataña
irikang pinggi siring udāsina, polihana nyayā

3: nyayanikang pakṣa kalih kunang pājar nikang pinggir siring,
angrungu yan sīma sasaṇḍan ndan awidhita ta sangkaning u

4: jar irika ta yan katmu sor i pakṣa samasānak i sīma tiga,
makādi mapañjyanawung harṣa, makahetu

5: tan hananing pramāṇa, yan pitung sang apañjyanawung harṣa
anaṇḍakĕn, muang asāmbawaning wruha, makādi

Plate 6, verso,
line 1: ng anadi kabhuktyanipun, matangnyan balawan pakṣāki santana mapañji saraṇa, muang sarowangnya, hetunya

2: n pinunga kmitana sang hyang ājñā haji jaya song, mratisu-
baddhakĕn pagĕh i pangrakṣa taṇḍa rakryan ri pa

3: kṣa sang apañji saraṇa, ri wruha sang apañji saraṇa prayatna
// o //

FERRY CHARTER

1358 A.D.

according to van Stein Callenfels, *Oudheidkundig Verslag* 1918 and Brandes-Krom, *Oud-Javaansche Oorkonden,* vol. II, 1913, p. 255.

Incomplete.

Plate 1, recto,

line *1*: swasti çrī çākawarsātīta 1280, çrawana māsa, tithi, pratipāda çuklapaksa, ha, u, ça, wāra madangkungan

2: aiçanyastha grahacāra, pusya naksatra, jīwadewatā, agneya mandala, bajra yoga, rodra muhūrtta, çaçī parwwe

3: ça, nāga karana, karkkata rāçī, irikā diwaçanyājñā pāduka çrī tiktawilwanagareçwara, çrī rājasanagara nāma rājabhise

4: ka, ranaprathita mantrinirjjita nrpāntaropayana surānggano-pamānāneka warakāminī sewyamāna, garbhotpatti nāma

5: dyah çrī hayāmwuruk, makamanggalyājñā pāduka bhatāra çrī tribhuwanottungga rājadewī jayawisnuwarddhanī nāma rājñy-ābhi

6: seka, nrtta racanādi guna koçalyālaya tīrthodakamaya nirmala-mānasa, sthāpita ngkāne nagare kahuripan, dyah çrī

Plate 1, verso,

line *1*: gītārjjā sāksad arddharājaparameçwarī, muang pāduka bha-tāra çrī krtawarddhana bhupālaka, sasyādi bhawa samrddhi-karana wrstisya

2: ndana sannibhārthajanasantusti prasūtijanakānawaratadāna, tumapĕl ākyā rājyāçrita, dyah çrī cakreçwara çrī hariwang-çawarddha

3: natara, sirāmrddhyakĕn santāna pratisantāna pāduka bhatāra çrī wisnuwarddhana, sang mokteng mandāragiri nhĕr saprawrtyācāra

4 : laksana bhatāra çrī wisnuwarddhana kta lana tinirutiru nirā
n jagatpālaka, tasmāt matangnyan alung aswö kta kadharme-
ṣṭan pādu

5 : ka bhaṭāra çrī kṛtawarddhana mahārāja, lakṣananira mangkana, yata dwāranirānganukāra nāma bhaṭāra çrī wiṣnuward-
dhana, ikang pa

6 : ñji sminingrāt, yugapat mwang ājñā pāduka bhaṭāra rājadewī
mahārājasa nāma rājñyābhiṣeka, kanaka maṇiratnā

. . . .

Plate 3, recto,
line 1 : mahārāja, tan kawuntat sang dharmmaprawaktā wyawahāra-
wiccedaka, samgĕt i tirwan, ḍang ācārya çiwanātha, makapadasthan sang āryya wa

2 : ngçādhipati, nyāyawyākaraṇaçāstra parisamāpta samgĕt i
manghuri, ḍang ācāryyāgreçwara, nyāyawyākaraṇaçāstra parisamāpta, samgĕt i

3 : kaṇḍamuhi, ḍang ācāryya jayasmara, sangkyaçāstraparisa-
māpta, samgĕt i pamwatan, ḍang ācāryya widyānātha nyāya
wyākaraṇaçāstrapa

4 : risamāpta, samgĕt i jambi, ḍang ācāryya çiwādhipa nyāya
wyākaraṇa çāstra parisamāpta, samgĕt i kaṇḍangan atuha,
ḍang ācāryya çrīghana,

5 : boddhatarkka parisamāpta, samgĕt i kaṇḍangan rare ḍang
ācāryya samatājñāna boddhatarkka parisamāpta, sarwwe ika
ta kabeh, kuṭā

6 : ramānawādi çāstra wiwecana tatpara, kapwa samasama çakte
kawiwākṣāning çāstra makādi kuṭāramānawa, makadon niçcaya jñāna

Plate 3, verso,
line 1 : ri nyāyānyāyani pakṣanikang wyawahārī kaliḥ, muwaḥ dharmmādhyakṣa ring kasogatan, pungkwī padlĕgan, ḍang ācārya
nādendra, boddha

2 : tarkka wyākaraṇaçāstra parisamāpta, makanaryyama, dharmmādhyakṣa ring kaçaiwan, nāma puṣpapāta, ḍang ācāryya
dharmmarāja, makapadasthan sa

3 : ng āryya rājaparākrama, mahādwija bhujangga sangrakṣana
dharmmādhyakṣa sangyojita, sinārabhāra pāduka çrī mahārāja dharmmādhyakṣa, maka

4: don karakṣan para pungku ring kaçaiwan, makādi mahādwija, i pingsornyājnā pāduka çrī mahārāja, kumonakĕn ikanang anambangi saya

5: wadwīpamaṇḍala, makādi pañji marggabhaya, makasikasir ajaran rata, sthapita, munggwi canggu, pagawayakna sang hyang ājñā haji praçā

6: sti, rājasanagaralañcaṇa, munggwe salaḥ sikining tāmra, riptopala, kapangkwa denikang anāmbangi sayawadwīpamaṇḍala, makā

. . . ` . . . .

Plate 5 (?), recto,

line 1: nuṣa, i tĕmon, parajĕngan, i pakaṭekan, i wunglu, i rabutri, i bañu mṛdu, i gocor, i tambak, i pujut,

2: i mirĕng, ing dmak, i klung, i pagḍangan, i mabuwur, i goḍong (?), i rumasan, i canggu, i raṇḍu gowok, i wahas, i nagara,

3: i sarba, i waringin pitu, i lagada, i pamotan, i tulangan, i panumbangan, i jruk, i trung, i kambang çrī, i tḍa, i gsang, i

4: bukul, i çūrabhaya, muwaḥ prakāraning naditīra pradeça sthānaning anāmbangi i maḍantĕn, i waringin wok, i bajrapura, i

5: sambo, i jerebeng, i pabulangan, i balawi, i luwayu, i katapang, i pagaran, i kamuḍi, i parijik, i parung, i pasi-

6: wuran, i kĕḍal, i bhangkal, i wiḍang, i pakbohan, i lowara (?), i ḍuri, i rāçi, i rewun, i tgalan, i dalangara, i

Plate 5 (?), verso,

line 1: sumbang, i malo, i ngijo, i kawangen, i suḍaḥ, i kukutu, i balun, i marĕbo, i turan, i jipang, i ngawi, i wangkalang,

2: i pnūḥ, i wulung, i barang, i pakatelan, i wareng, ing amban, i kĕmbu, i wulayu, sarwwe, ika ta kabeh, nadītīrapradeça, sthā

3: nanya ng anambangi sayawadwīpamaṇḍala, ngūnikālanyānghyang ājñā haji praçāsti, rājasanagaralañcaṇa, kunĕng tingkah ikang a

4: nambangi sayawadwīpamaṇḍala, makādi pañji mārggabhaya, kyajaran rata, mwang pañjyangrakṣāji, kyajaran rāgi, kewala swatantrā, ta

5: n kaparabyāpāra, tan katamāna deni winawa sang māna katrīṇi, lwīrnya, pangkur, tawan, tirip, salwiraning nāyaka, parttaya, apinghe,

6 : akurug, awajuh, wadihadi, sapuṇḍuḥnya kabeh makāding raweḥ lawan sahananing mangilala dṛwya haji, wuluwulu parawu

. . . .

Plate 9, recto,

line 1 : pikulpikulanya, ri sawulu ning dwal, ikang samangka ikang tan knana dṛwya haji, yapwan lĕwiḥ sakeng pahinga, knana lĕwiḥnya de sang makĕ

2 : kĕranya, sodhara haji tan adhikana, muwaḥ kinawnangakĕnya ng anambangi sayawadwīpamaṇḍala, ri kālani kapūjān sang hyang ājñā ha

3 : ji praçāsti wnang angadwa sawung nīta, jūḍi, acuringa kinang-syan ri kālanyāmūjā daçārddha diwaça purwwapara ri kālani kapūjān sang hyang ājñā

4 : haji praçāsti, kunĕng sangka ri gĕngnyādhimuktinikang anām-bangi sayawadwīpamaṇḍala makādi pañji marggabhaya, mwang pañjyangrakṣāji, kyajaran

5 : rāgi, sthāpita, mungwi trung, manghanakĕn ta pamūjāngkĕn sārini puṣpanyānghaturakĕn sambaḥ ri sang hyang ājña haji praçāsti, 400 ring sara

6 : hi mijil angkĕn pūrṇnamāning āṣāḍa, muwaḥ anugraha pāduka çrī mahārāja yan hana dāçadāçī bharyyopabhāryya

Plate 9, verso,

line 1 : kunĕng asing awakanya, swāmigata, lungha sangke swāminya, tan bwatana ktekang anambangy angĕntasakĕn sangkeng nadī-tīra, yadin sā

2 : dhu prawṛttinya ng anambangi, kalut sangkeng aṣṭacora, muwaḥ yan hana strī karĕm asing awakanya, kasambut ta ya denya ng anambangi tan sa

3 : nggahĕn strīsanggrahaṇa ktekang anambangy angĕntasakĕn anambut iriya, muwaḥ yan hana wwang kapūrwwarṇan tinam-bangan aweḥ ta

4 : yeng anambangy asing awakani pawehanya, yadyapin oliha-nyānyāya, ikang pawehnya, tan doṣana tekang anambangi ta

5 : n sanggahĕn ananggapi duṣṭa, muwaḥ ri sdĕnganikang anam-bangi, amwata paḍatining akalang, dagangan asing awakanya, karĕm pwekang daga

112 CHARTERS

6: ngan, tan bwatana tekang anambangi, ndatan wehana ta ya tambangan yan çīrṇekang dagangan, muwaḥ yan ha

Plate 10, recto,

line 1: na dṛwya kely asing awakanya, kasambut pwa ya denyang anambangi, tan doṣana tekang anambangy amalaku phala çramanyānambut angrakṣa,

2: ndan sapawehnyang adṛwya tanggapĕn ya, mangkanānugraha çrī mahārāja irikang anambangi sayawadwīpa, makādyajaran rata, paçcat,

3: ring wkasan, manghaturakĕn sambaḥ tekang anāmbangi saya-wadwīpamaṇḍala, makādi pañji mārggabhaya, kyajaran rata, mwang

4: pañjyangrakṣāji, aneka mahārghyawastrapramukhanamaskara, ikang aneka wastrāngkĕn sārini puṣpanyānghaturakĕn sa

5: mbaḥ ri lbū pāduka çrī mahārāja, sangka ri gĕngnyādhimuk-tinikang anambangi, wineh akmitana sang hyang ājñā haji praçāsti, rā

6: jasanagaralañcana, muwaḥ rakryan mantri katrīṇi, sinungan pasök-pasök, sayathākrama, muwaḥ rakryan dĕmung

Plate 10, verso,

line 1: rakryan kanuruhan, rakryan rangga, rakryan tumĕnggung, kapwa wineḥ pasök-pasök, sayathākrama, makanaryyama, sang dharmmādhya

2: kṣa ring kaçaiwan sang dharmmādhyakṣa ring kasogatan kap-wa wineḥ pasök-pasök, sayathākrama, sang dharmmopapatti samudāya, kapwa

3: wineḥ pasök-pasök, sayathākrama, makaphala, mratisubad-dhākn ānugraha pāduka çrī mahārāja, irikang anambangi sayawadwī

4: pamaṇḍala, makādi pañji mārggabhaya, kyajaran rata, mwang pañjyangrakṣāji, kyajaran rāgi, tlas labdhāpagĕḥ, kunĕng yan hana u

5: mulahulaḥ sarasa sang hyang ājñā haji praçāsti, kmitanikang anambangi sayawadwīpamaṇḍala, makādi pañji mārggabhaya, kya

6: jaran rata, mwang pañjyangrakṣāji, kyajaran rāgi, nguniweh yan panglbura kaswatantranikang anambangi sayawadwīpa-maṇḍala, a

CHARTER OF BATUR

according to Bosch, *Oudheidkundig Verslag* 1915.

Fragmentary.

I. Large fragment, recto,

line 1: sambarasamartthya, rakryyan apatih ring kahuripan mpu
taṇḍing, nayawinaya guṇānurūpantah purarakṣa

2: mun mpu kapat çūrasapatnamarddana, rakryan kanuruhan
mpu pakis wairibala wirāntaka, rakryan

3: ma ripusangkyapranāça rakryan tuměnggung mpu nala sādu-
rakṣanāsādunikramatatpara, makapuraya

4: ngala kaḍiri mpu mada raṇamaddyāryyanukulakaraṇa, para-
sainyaçirah, kapalagandotpana ma

5: yandikopāyasamartthya, sākṣāt praṇāla mratisubaddaken pa-
ṇḍiri çrī mahārāja siniwi ring sayawadwīpama

6: pantara, makanaryyama sang nyāyānyāyawyawahārawiccha-
daka, sang. pamgět i tiruan, ḍang ācāryya çi

I. Large fragment, verso,

line 1: karaṇaçāstraparisamāpta, samgět i kaṇḍamohi ḍang ācāryya
marmmanātha, nyāyawyakaraṇaçāstraparisa

2: ri ḍang ācāryya smaranātha, nyāyawyakaraṇaçāstraparisamāpta, samgět i kaṇḍangan rare, ḍang ācāryya mahā

3: wyakaraṇaçāstraparisamāpta, samgět i jambi, smaranātha,
nyāyawyakaraṇaçāstraparisamāpta, samgět i pamua

4: greçwara, nyāyawyakaraṇaçāstraparisamāpta, ḍarmmadyakṣa
ring kaçaiwan, sang āryya harṣarāja, ḍang

5: nyāyawyakaraṇaçāstraparisamāpta, ḍarmmadyakṣa ring kasogatan, sang āryyādirāja, ḍang ācāryya

6: rtta wyakaraṇatantraparisamāpta, kuněng padartthanyājñā
pāduka çrī mahārāja kumonakěn i para

II. Middlesized fragment, recto,
line *1*:   rika ta sang hyang maṇḍale sāgara, iringĕn tkap sang hyang
     2:   ra kramanira ring puhun malama, tumuruna labupanaya
     3:   ni kapujan sang hyang kabuyutan i kalyasĕm, asuji
     4:   tkap sang hyang maṇḍale kaṇḍawa ri talun i wasana ri *sa*
     5:   tapwānuwuna kalasa pataraṇa maguta payung sa
     6:   s karuhun kadīrgghyayuṣan pāduka çrī mahārāja

II. Middlesized fragment, verso,
line *1*:   sang hyang maṇḍale sāgara, kunĕng ring caitramāsa, pañcada
     2:   maṇḍale sāgara, iringĕn tkap sang hyang maṇḍale talun
     3:   para kakyatunggu batur i talun makadon enaka
     4:   duta çrī mahārāja, mangkana rasani panghayubagya pādu
     5:   ha, kunĕng tingkaha para kakyangiringa ri sang hyang maṇḍa-
          la npa
     6:   ya pariçudḍa, tumutakna palupwi sang sidda puru panguni,
          ma

III. Small fragment, recto,
          han bhadrapadamasa, pañcadaçi çuklapak
          ri sang hyang kabuyutan ing kalihan kapwa tu
          le sa bon tra

III. Small fragment, verso,
          tan hananing wiroḍa ri dlāha
          tanpangucapakna salah kna kewala patĕha ri

CHARTERS OF BILULUK

according to van Stein Callenfels, *Oudheidkundig Verslag* 1918.

I

Charter of 1366 A.D.

Recto,

line 1: hiku suratingong, kagugona dene si samasanak ing biluluk,
rehane wnang acibukana bañu asin, tatkāla pūjāne pisan

2: satahun, hawalĕra sapĕkĕn, hapan iku wnang katama ktmu hing
kunakuna, tanpa dola ta hiya tanpa weweha, adol po

3: hiya haweweh, kaḍĕṇḍaha ta hiya dening panampan saḍĕṇḍa-
ning amomoṭot, hana po dene pamūjāne, 300, nangkĕ

4: n tahun, panangkane mĕtu saking aḍapur, pagagarĕme, ku, 7,
nangkĕn wulan, hiku kawruhane si paraḍapur ing pinggir
samadāya

Verso,

line 1: makanguni kang aḍapur ing majapahit, siwihos kunĕng yan
hanangrubuhakna wangçaningong kang biluluk, kang tanggulunan, a

2: mangguha pāpa, sanghyang trayodaçasakṣi amatyanana, den-
tāmatyanana, yan humalintang ring tgal, sahutĕn dening ulā
mandī yan ma

3: reng alas dmakning mong, manglangkahana mingmang, yan
mareng bañwagöng sahutĕn denin wuhaya, mumul, tuwiran,
yan liwat ing hawan göng kasopa wu

4: languna, yan hudan sambĕrĕn ing glap, yan haneng umahnya
katibānāgni tanpa warṣa, liputĕn gsĕngana de hyang agni
wehĕn bhasmibhūta saha dṛ

5: wyanya, tanpanoliha ring wuntat, tarung ring adgan, tampyal
i kiwan uwah ī tngĕnan, tutuḥ tuṇḍuhnya, blaḥ kapalanya,
sbit wtĕngnya, tatas ḍaḍa

6: nya, wtwakĕn ḍalĕmanya, pangan dagingnya, inum rahnya,
at-hĕr pĕpĕdakĕn wehi prāṇantika, bwangakĕn ing akaça, tiba-
kĕn ing kawaḥ, astu, i çaka 1288.

II

Charter of 1391 A. D.

Recto,

line 1 : Hiku wruhane si parajuru ning asambewara, samadaya, yen andikaningong, amagĕhakĕn andikanira tala

2 : mpakanira pāduka bhaṭāra çrī parameçwara sira sang mokta ring wiṣṇubhawana, dene kaluluputane si parawangça ring

3 : biluluk, asambewara sarwwa papat, hadagang, hamahat, hajagal, hamalantĕn, hamdĕl, hamutĕr, hanglakṣa hanga

4 : pu, mangkana maniḥ kang atunggu kasiman, asambewara, sarwwa tunggal, hiku ta luputa ring arikpuriḥ saprakara, padadaḥ, pawiwāha,

Verso,

line 1 : patatar, pasadran, byangkatan, palalandĕp, palalajĕr, pararajĕg, pabata, pabale, parahab, pasusuk, parawuhan,

2 : luputing titiban, sahang, cabe, kumukus, kapulaga, wsi, kawali wsi, pinggan, pangjālin, kapas, makanguni tahil paduging luputa, ndan ta knaha ring pa

3 : mihos, malĕr, anuta rehe kang sajiwajiwa, limangatus ing wong tunggal, makadon anaha si parajuru hanagiha pĕpĕk i rehane marĕkeringong, lawan dene

4 : jajakane, sasangkulane, kaponakane, kang amahat ing biluluk i rehane luputĕn tahil jajalukan sangu pangisi kaṇḍi, kang rājamudra yen uwus kawaca

5 : kagugona dene si parawangça ring biluluk, titi ka, 2, i çaka 1313.

III

Charter of 1395 A. D.

Recto,

line 1 : hiku wruhane kang anampak tahil ing ananaṇḍa hananaṇḍu, hatuku latĕk, sakalwiraning anampak

2 : yen andikaningong, dene si parawangça ring biluluk, ring tanggulunan, i rehane luputa ring tahil ing ananaṇḍa

3 : hananaṇḍu, hatuku latĕk, luputa, makadona po hana hanagiha tahil ing ananaṇḍu, hananaṇḍu, hatuku

4 : latĕk, ing parawangça ring biluluk, ring tanggulunan, i rehane marĕka iringong, aja, den sidigawe

5 : si parawangça ring biluluk, ring tanggulunan, kang rājamudra yen uwus kawaca, kagugona dene si pa

6 : rawangça ring biluluk, tithi, māsa jyastha, i çaka 1317.

CHARTER OF RĔNĔK

1379 A.D.

according to Stutterheim and Pigeaud,
Een Javaansche Oorkonde uit den Bloeitijd van Madjapahit,
Djawa, vol. 6, 1926.

———

Plate I, recto,
line 1: wontĕn andikānira nalāmpakānira bhaṭāra ring wĕngkĕr.
angūlihakna bhūmīnira samasanak ing rĕ
2: nĕk, kang kaladan dening akuwu ring tāmbak, gunging sawaḥ,
tgal, jöng 4, kilĕs ujak uring, punika ta sāmpun
3: mantuk denira sang āryya gunāndikā, sira sang kinon açraḥha
denira sang āryya maring sawaḥ, sira pañji gobe
4: r, sira pañji harṣa lĕwiḥ, sira gĕnti ri handon, kabayan ing
atuha sira mantrī narotama sira mnĕng, 4, puni

Plate I, verso,
line 1: ka tta punang açraḥ, tgal, i sira samasanak hing rĕnĕk,
bhūmī siring hañjĕnĕngi, wragaji pañangan, sira
2: budḍa kabayan, sira pupon, juburuḥ sira blang, wwang, 3,
ring talaga, sira buyut umpĕk, sira darana, sira bade
3: , wwang, 3, wadāna ring pamanggihan, sira juru tangsor, sira
juru madāya, sira malambangan, sira sunduk, wwang, 3,
4: sira parawangça hañjĕnĕngi, sira samasanak ring mangĕnĕb,
sira mūladharmma pagon, sira rubung, wwang, 3, sira
5: samasanak, ring pagĕr, sira mūladharmma guṇita, sira blang,
sira soma, wwang, 3, makādhī pawiḍigan

Plate II, recto,
line 1: sira samasanak ring gilang, sira mūladharmma guṇa, sira
gusti rañca, sira malar, wwang, 3, samering lĕmbaḥ

2 : lawadan, sira buyut sangū, sira wita, sira tukup, wwang, 3,
kapalang, sira tanggon, kabaya

3 : n, sira kĕṭul, gusti sira biṣa, wwang, 3, makādhī wadana, sira
sang anden ing tāmbak, sira gampil

4 : hangalihi sira bungkĕm, mantĕn, sira gajul, juburuḥ sira donan, sira pagon, sira surung,

5 : , wwang, 6, puniku tta kang katulis hañjĕnĕngi samangarĕp,
ring sadeçadeça, punang wong lĕmbaḥ,

Plate II, verso,

line 1 : hamalĕrakĕn yen bhūmī wragaji, sira parajinuru, sira parawangça ring wragaji, sama malĕrakĕn ye

2 : n bhūmīnira samasanak ring rĕnĕk, puniku tta sāmpun kapa-
sĕk kapagĕhan, pirak satak,

3 : ring sadeçadeça, makādhī likittabhukti, kapangan kenum
denira sang añjĕnĕngi, samadāya,

4 : keh ing deça hañjĕnĕngi, 9, tithī, wa, pang, ba, ka, 9, çīrāh 1
tulisira kanuruhan sira pa

5 : raçī.

CHARTER OF WALAṆḌIT

1381/1405 A.D.

according to Brandes, *Notulen van de Directievergaderingen van het Bataviaasch Genootschap van Kunsten en Wetenschappen,* vol. 37, 1899, p. 64.

———

Recto,

line 1: wruhanekānglakoni hanagiḥ titilöman, ring walaṇḍit, yen andikaningong, de

2: ne kang deça hing walaṇḍit, mamanggis lili, jĕbing, kacaba, i rehane luwara dene ha

3: nagiḥ titilöman, i rehe kang deça i walaṇḍit deça ilahila, hulun hyangira sang hyang

4: gunung brahmā, iku ta hawalöra sakwehing wong sakahuban dening deça i walaṇḍit, ta

5: n katagiha titilöman, ayo tinatab i rehing deça ilaila, kang rājamudra ye

Verso,

line 1: n uwus kawaca, kagugona dene kang wong walaṇḍit, tithi masa, 5, çirah 3, // i çakakala

2: 1327, asadamāsa, tithi, nawamikṛṣṇapakṣa, pa, ra, wara dungulan, irika diwasanya ri parawa

3: rgga ri walaṇḍit tinambrakĕn rājamūdra indikani talāmpaka-nira bhaṭāra hyang wkasing suka, i reha deça ila

4: ila hulun hyangira sang hyang gunung brahmā, yata kanimi-taning tinambrakĕn dening kabayan made, buyut....

5: ....

———

CHARTER OF PATAPAN

1385 A.D.

according to van Stein Callenfels, *Oudheidkundig Verslag* 1918.

Recto,

line 1: // o // surat sang āryya rājaparākrama, dang ācāryya wiçwa-
nātha, rawuha kang para sāme ing

2: patapan, sakehing raramātuha nom, makangūni buyut, wru-
haning para sāme ing pata

3: pan, yen ana rājamudra handikanira talāmpakanira bhaṭāra
hyang wiçesa hamagěhakěn andikanira talā

4: mpakanira bhaṭāra sang mokta ring paring mālaya dening
janggan ing patapan i rehaning sumalahe sahana

Verso,

line 1: kirā mpu .... janggan tumrapa satkaning pañlěk,
hanut rasaning rājamudra, iku ta suma

2: laha tĕkanin kubon, sawaḥ, makangūni pomahan, tithī jyeṣṭa.
çirah 7 // o //

CHARTER OF KARANG BOGĔM

1387 A.D.

according to van Stein Callenfels, *Oudheidkundig Verslag* 1918.

———

Recto,

line 1: iku wruhane para mantrīng tirah āryya songga pabayĕman āryya carita, purut, patiḥ lajĕr, wruhane yen ingong amagĕ

2: hakĕn karange patiḥ tamba karang bogĕm, penganane kidul lĕbuḥ penganane wetan sadawata anutug sāgara pisan

3: penganane kulon babatane dmung wana, anutug sāgara pisan, pasawahane sajung babatan sakikil, iku ta malĕra haja den siddhigawe,

4: hana ta kawulaningong saking grĕsik warigaluh ahutang sakṭi rong lakṣa gnĕp sabisane hasikĕp rowang warigaluḥ luputa ta pangarah saking si

5: ddhayu kapangarahan po hiya saki dalĕm galangan kawolu anghaturakna ta hiya hacan bobot sewu sarahi atambak sesine

6: tambake kahature ringong, hana tādagang, angogogoṇḍok, amahat, luputa ta ring arik puriḥ saprakara, knaha ta hiya ring pamūja

Verso,

satĕngah, anuta sararataning wargga taman sabhumi, tithi, ka 7, çirah 8 // andaka kakatang //

———

CHARTER OF KATIDEN

1392 A.D.

according to Poerbatjaraka, *Tijdschrift van het Bataviaasch Genootschap van Kunsten en Wetenschappen*, vol. 76, 1936, p. 387.

Recto,

line 1: iku wruhane si para same salurah wetaning kawi sakuloning bañu, sawetaning bañu, pa-

2: ra waddhana, juru, buyut, makanguni pacataṇḍa hi turen, yen ingong hamagěhakěn ha

3: ndikanira talampakanira pāduka bhaṭāra çrī parameçwara sira sang mokta ring wiṣṇubhawana, handikani

4: ra sira sang mokta ring kṛttabhuwana, dene kapūrwastitine si para same ri katiḍen

5: kasawlas deça, i rehe hangrakṣa halalang i gunung lějar, luputa ri saprakara luputa

6: ring jalang palawang, takěr turun, makanguni tahil sakal-wiraning titisara luputa, makanguni

Verso,

line 1: dening alas kakayu gaten hantiganing pasiran, tan ananing anglarangana hi rehi tan wnang

2: larangana, tan ananin aningkah-aningkuha, kang rajamudra yen uwus kawaca kagugona dene

3: kang deça hi lumpang, titi ka 1, i çaka 1317.

CHARTER OF SHELA MAṆḌI

1394, 1395, 1396 A.D.

according to Cohen Stuart, *Kawi Oorkonden*, 1875, p. 11.

———

Plate 1, recto,
line 1: iku wruhane si para same sahuman, pagĕr, para wadanā, buyut ing gĕsang, hasḍahan tani hi tĕrung, pa
2: tih nadi, paca taṇḍa hi tĕrung, haryya wisanā, makanguni hangucap gawe tani ring majapahit, haryya
3: warani, yen andikaningong, dene bhūmine si darani, kang ing çela maṇḍi, sabhumine si darani,
4: kang ing çela maṇḍi, i rehane luputa ring palawang tahil, sakalwiraning rājakaryya, titiban,
5: titisarā, rarawuhan, harik purih saprakara saki dalĕm, hadĕg ringgita, amitanā,
6: i çakā 1316, amuktiha hing açirah pitu, hawalĕra ta sabhūmine si dara

Plate 1, verso,
line 1: ni kadĕg, ringgita, tan alonga, tan awuwuha, tan pangladana bhūmine brayane, tan kala
2: danā, iku ta wukating (?) pagagalihane hing katanen, satkani rājamūdra, kang rājamū
3: dra yen uwus, kawacā, kagugona dene si darani, titi, ka, rpa (?), i çakā 1316,
4: hantukira rĕrambĕkĕl, tuwuh, tan ikut, sawahira darani. ring çela maṇḍi, kajnĕngan denira
5: para binuyut ing çela maṇḍi, sira sang aryya .... mbu .... uyut (?), angarĕp sira janana, sira buyut, sĕngguh, kaba
6: yan sira kol (?), pañarikan sira sambarana, sira rangga glar, hantuk ira para binuyut amalĕrakĕn buminira da
7: rani .... i sawah jöng, 1, ki, 1, jara, 1, hiring, 1, ...ĕ........

Plate 2, recto,

line 1: iku wruhane kang wong hangalap, bumine si darani, ri çela maṇḍi, kang pabuyutan, yen andika

2: ningong, tan anani wong pati-pati hangalapa saking babaneh hawalĕra sabumine si darani kang si

3: ma salawang, tan pangladana tan kaladana, i rehe huwus katuri (*buri* ?) ringong, iku ta kang angrakṣa

4: sapiha, sawine kadahuta tumuli satkaning rājamūdra, hawalĕra kang sabumine si darani kang sima

5: salawang kadahuta sawine, makadona hiya ngamekṣakna (?) hangalapa, i rehane kaḍĕṇḍaha saki dalĕm

6: saḍĕṇḍani pangalap (?) bumi dalĕm, ḍĕṇḍahane, kang rājamūdra yen uwus kawaca kagugona dene si darani pihagmane,

7: titi, ka 2 (*3* ?), i çaka 1317,

Plate 2, verso,

line 1: iku wruhane kang apangarah putajenan, sakalwiraning wong apangarah putajenan, yen a

2: ndikaningong, dene kasimane si darani kang desa ring çela (*ma*) ṇḍi, i rehane luputa ring putajenan,

3: sakalwiraning putajenan, saki dalĕm, saki yawi, luput, luput ing ririmbagan, pabata, titisara,

4: rarawuhan, titiban, jajalukan, susuguhan, pangisi kaṇḍi, luput ing sosorohan,

5: garĕm, hurugurugan dalan, bĕbnĕraning canggu, sakalwiraning rājakaryya putajenan, saki dalĕm, saki yawi

6: luputa, luput ing arik purih saprakara, kang rajamūdra yen uwus kawaca kagugona dene si darani pihagmane

7: titi, ka .... i çakā, 1318.

THREE MEN OF THE COMMON PEOPLE, V. PAGE V.

Printed in the USA
CPSIA information can be obtained
at www.ICGtesting.com
LVHW042325051023
759999LV00027B/898